Thai Sin Cookbook:

Quick and easy authentic Thai recipes to make at home

DINGO
BOOK CLUB

"Great Books Change Life"

Table of Contents

4

Introduction

Thai cuisine has gained fame across the world because of its unique taste and flavors. If you are someone who loves Thai cuisine and wants to learn authentic Thai recipes, then you have come to the right place.

The popularity of Thai food has no boundaries. Thai food can be simpler to make when compared to other cuisines, but you will need to follow all the steps, as it is an intense process. The demand for Thai food is such that there are Thai restaurants across the world. Thanks to this book, you can now prepare these lip-smacking recipes at home instead of eating Thai food at a restaurant.

This book contains 75 different recipes that are simple to make and delicious. All of these are authentic Thai recipes, and if you follow every step mentioned for each recipe, you will create a dish that has the same aroma and unique taste that a traditional Thai dish should have. There is a possibility that you may be unable to source some of the ingredients mentioned, but you can use substitutes for those and will still obtain an authentic Thai dish.

So what are we waiting for? Have fun cooking different Thai dishes.

An Introduction to Thai Food

Thai food is one of the most loved cuisines from across the world. Thai food is delicious and packed with many flavors, which can make people think that the cuisine is complex. On the contrary, Thai food is easy and simple to make. If you want to start cooking Thai food at home, there are a few necessary ingredients and cooking equipment you will need in your kitchen.

Essential Ingredients

Thai Fish Sauce

Thai Fish sauce, known as nam pla, is a pungent seasoning that is made from fermenting or cooking fish in salt. When you purchase this ingredient, ensure that the sauce only contains anchovies, salt, and water. You must use it sparingly since it has more than 500 mg sodium per spoon.

Curries

Curries are an essential component of Thai cuisine. Most people choose to buy curry pastes from the market. There are a variety of red and green curry pastes that can be found. If you prefer making curry paste, follow the recipes given in the next chapter.

Vinegar

Unseasoned rice vinegar, along with lime, adds sourness to any salad dressing. It is used in most dipping sauces. If you do not have unseasoned rice vinegar, you can use cider vinegar as a substitute.

Coconut Milk

Coconut milk is used in most Thai curries, and it is made by extracting milk from coconut flesh using warm water. You can use canned coconut milk if you do not want to spend time making coconut milk. If you want to reduce the number of calories in your dish, you can dilute coconut milk with warm water or use a "lite" version of the milk.

Rice

Glutinous rice or sticky rice is a staple in Thailand and is eaten like bread. You can choose Jasmine rice or whole-grain rice like black sticky rice or brown jasmine rice.

Chile Peppers

The heat in Thai food comes from fresh and dried chile peppers. Dried red chilies are used in curry pastes and add spice to stir fries or soups. Serrano, jalapeno, or cayenne chilies are often used in curries.

Lime

Lime leaves and juice are often used in salads, fried rice, and grilled meats. The former is often difficult to come by; therefore, you can use lime zest to add a citrusy aroma to soups and curries.

Garlic and Shallots

Garlic and grilled shallots are added to most salads, stir fries, and curries. The latter adds a little crunch to the dish while the former adds a beautiful flavor to the dish.

Essential Equipment

Thai home cooking does not require many tools unless you decide to make a traditional Thai dish. You can make most "authentic" Thai dishes using the tools you have in your kitchen.

Mortar and Pestle

Curry paste is an essential ingredient in Thai cuisine and most newbies trying to make basic Thai dishes will start off with making some kind of paste. Herbs and spices are pounded in a mortar to add flavor and to extract oils that enhance the flavor of the dish. You can make small quantities of paste using a mortar and pestle.

Rice Cooker

As mentioned earlier, rice is an integral part of Thai cuisine. It is used in every food cart, restaurant, eatery, and household. It is practical to use a rice cooker since it is an efficient way to cook rice. You have to only add water and rice to the cooker and turn on the switch. Rice will be ready in no time.

Wok or Skillet

It is good to have a carbon-steel skillet or wok in your kitchen. Skillets are used to deep fry or stir-fry some ingredients.

Citrus Juicer

This equipment does not need to be in the kitchen, but it is a nice tool to have. Lime is a source of acidity in most Thai dishes. A citrus juicer will make the task easier for you.

Now that we have looked at some of the common ingredients and equipment you need in your kitchen, let us take a look at some common cooking techniques.

Cooking Techniques

Stir Frying

Stir-frying is a fuss-free and a quick way of cooking. Place a skillet on medium heat and oil to it. When the oil is hot, add your ingredients and stir them quickly to heat them thoroughly. Once the vegetables are cooked, transfer them to a plate and serve hot. Since stir-frying is a quick process, you must prepare your ingredients before you start cooking.

Stewing

Stewing is one of the best cooking techniques since the ingredients retain all the natural sweetness and goodness. Cut the ingredients into smaller pieces and cover them up with enough liquid. Cover the pot and cook on low heat so the ingredients cook slowly.

Steaming

Ingredients are cooked by the vapors that rise from the liquid that is boiling below. Since the ingredients do not come in contact with the liquid, most nutrients are retained. It is best to use fresh ingredients to get the best out of steaming.

Deep Frying

Deep-frying can be done in a deep pan or wok. In this method, food is cooked in large amounts of oil. It is important to measure the temperature of the cooking oil. If the oil is too hot, the ingredients will burn and if the oil is not hot enough, the ingredients will not be cooked fully.

Chapter 1:

Thai Curry Paste Recipes

Thai cuisine is incomplete without the authentic curry pastes. Here are the most commonly used curry pastes, made from scratch. These curry pastes can be used in meat, soups, noodles, rice, etc.

Thai Red Curry Paste

Preparation Time: 10 minutes

Cooking Time: 10 minutes

Ingredients:

- ½ cup purple onion or shallots, chopped
- 3-4 red chilies or 3-4 teaspoon Thai chili sauce
- 4 inches galangal or ginger, sliced
- 2 stalks fresh lemongrass minced or 6 tablespoons frozen lemongrass
- 8 cloves garlic, peeled, sliced
- 4 tablespoons tomato puree of tomato ketchup
- 1 ½ teaspoons coriander, ground
- 2 teaspoon cumin, ground
- 2-3 teaspoons chili powder or to taste
- ½ teaspoon white pepper powder
- ½ teaspoon cinnamon powder (optional)
- 2 teaspoons shrimp paste
- 6 tablespoons thick coconut milk
- 4 tablespoons fish sauce
- 2 teaspoons sugar
- ¼ cup fresh lemon juice

Method:

1. Add all the ingredients except coconut milk into a mortar and pound with a pestle into a paste.

2. When it is pounded into a paste, add coconut milk and mix well. If it is too thick, add some more coconut milk. If you don't have a mortar and a pestle, add all the ingredients in a food processor and blend until a paste is achieved.

3. Transfer into an airtight container. Refrigerate until use for up to 10-12 days or freeze for up to 3 months.

Thai Green Curry Paste

Preparation Time: 10 minutes

Cooking Time: 10 minutes

Ingredients:

- 20 green chilies, chopped
- 2 onions, chopped
- 2 cups cilantro leaves, chopped
- Juice of a lemon

- 12 cloves garlic, peeled
- 1 ½ inch galangal or ginger, peeled, sliced
- Zest of 2 lemons, grated
- 2 tablespoons ground coriander
- 4 tablespoons ground cumin
- 4 stalks lemongrass, minced
- Salt to taste
- ½ teaspoon pepper powder

Method:

1. Add the ingredients into a mortar and pound with a pestle into a paste.

2. When it is pounded into a paste, add a little water and mix well. If it is too thick, add some more water. If you don't have a mortar and a pestle, add all the ingredients in a food processor and blend with a little water until a paste is achieved.

3. Transfer into an airtight container. Refrigerate until use for up to 10-12 days or freeze up to 3 months.

Thai Yellow Curry Paste

Preparation Time: 10 minutes

Cooking Time: 10 minutes

Ingredients:

- 2 stalks lemongrass, minces or 4 tablespoons frozen lemongrass
- 4 shallots, sliced
- 8 cloves garlic
- 4 yellow chilies, sliced (or 4 red chilies)
- 4 inches galangal or ginger, sliced
- 2 teaspoons ground coriander
- 1 teaspoon cumin seeds
- 2 teaspoons ground cumin
- 1 ½ teaspoons turmeric
- ½ teaspoon cinnamon powder
- 2/3 teaspoon white pepper
- 4 tablespoon fish sauce
- 2 tablespoons lime juice
- 1 tablespoon shrimp paste or 1 tablespoon extra fish sauce
- 4 tablespoons brown sugar
- 2/3 can coconut milk or as required

- 2 tablespoons tomato ketchup (or 2 tablespoons tomato paste +1 teaspoon sugar)

Method:

1. Add the ingredients except coconut milk into a mortar and pound with a pestle into a paste.

2. When it is pounded into a paste, add coconut milk and mix well. If it is too thick, add some more coconut milk. If you don't have a mortar and a pestle add all the ingredients in a food processor and blend until a paste is achieved.

3. Transfer into an airtight container. Refrigerate until use up to 10-12 days or freeze up to 3 months.

Massaman Curry Paste

Preparation Time: 10 minutes

Cooking Time: 10 minutes

Ingredients:

- ½ cup peanuts, dry roasted
- 4 red chilies, dried
- 4-6 tablespoons lemongrass, minced, frozen
- 4 shallots, minced
- 10 cloves garlic, peeled
- 4 inches galangal or ginger, thinly sliced
- 2 teaspoons ground coriander
- 1 teaspoon whole cumin seeds
- 1 tablespoon ground cumin
- 2 teaspoons brown sugar or palm sugar
- ¼ teaspoon cinnamon, ground
- ¼ teaspoon ground cloves
- ¼ teaspoon ground nutmeg
- ½ teaspoon ground cardamom
- 2 teaspoons shrimp paste
- 4 tablespoons fish sauce
- Coconut milk, as required

Method:

1. Add the ingredients except coconut milk into a mortar and pound with a pestle into a paste.

2. When it is pounded into a paste, add a little coconut milk and mix well. If it is too thick, add some more water. If you don't have a mortar and a pestle add all the ingredients in a food processor and blend with a little coconut milk until a paste is achieved.

3. To make sauce, increase the coconut milk.

4. Transfer into an airtight container. Refrigerate until use up to . 10-12 days or freeze up to 3 months.

Panang Curry Paste (Nam Prik Kaeng Phanaeng)

Preparation Time: 10 minutes

Cooking Time: 10 minutes

Ingredients:

For dry ingredients:

- 4 teaspoons roasted coriander seeds
- 6 pieces roasted mace
- 4 pods roasted cardamom
- 1 teaspoon peppercorns
- 1 teaspoon roasted cumin
- 1 teaspoon salt
- 6 mild green chili pepper, roasted
- 24 big dried red chilies, deseeded and soaked in water for 20 minutes, finely chopped

For fresh ingredients:

- 4 teaspoons galangal or ginger, peeled, chopped
- 2 teaspoons kaffir lime peel, chopped
- 6 tablespoons shallots, chopped
- 2 teaspoons shrimp paste
- 4 tablespoons lemongrass, chopped
- 4 tablespoons garlic, crushed

Method:

1. Add all the dry ingredients into a mortar and pound with a pestle. Pound until coarsely powdered.

2. Add the fresh ingredients into the dry ingredients or separate from? and pound until smooth. Alternately blend together all the ingredients in a food processor until smooth, adding a little water.

3. Transfer to an airtight container. Refrigerate until use, up to 10-12 days or freeze up to 3 months.

Chapter 2:

Snacks and Starters

Mu Ping (Grilled Pork on Skewers)

Serves: 4

Nutritional values per serving:

Calories – 132.2, Fat – 5.6 g, Carbohydrate – 3.6 g, Protein – 15.8 g

Preparation Time: 4 hours

Cooking Time: 15 minutes

Ingredients:

- 2 tablespoons cilantro roots or stems, preferably roots, finely chopped
- 4 cloves garlic cloves, peeled

- ½ tablespoon white peppercorns
- 2.5 pounds pork shoulder, cut against the grain into ½ inch pieces
- 4-5 tablespoons palm sugar, finely grated or melted in microwave
- 1 tablespoon light soy sauce
- ½ teaspoon baking powder, to tenderize meat (optional)
- 6 tablespoons coconut milk to brush the beef while grilling
- 1 ½ tablespoons fish sauce
- 1 tablespoon oyster sauce
- Bamboo skewers soaked in water for 2-3 hours

Method:

1. Pound together the cilantro roots, garlic, and white pepper in a mortar with a pestle.
2. Place the pork pieces in a bowl. Add the rest of the ingredients to the pounded mixture. Mix well. Place in the refrigerator to marinate for 3-4 hours.
3. Insert pork on to the bamboo skewers.
4. Grill on hot coals (or on a rack on the grill?). Baste with coconut milk. Turn the skewers every 2 minutes. Grill until the pork pieces are lightly charred on the outside and well-cooked inside.
5. Serve hot with Jaew (dried red chili dip).

Fried Prawns with White Pepper and Garlic

Serves: 8

Nutritional values per serving:

Calories – 377, Fat – 24.7 g, Carbohydrate – 19.5 g, Protein – 19.5 g

Preparation Time: 10 minutes

Cooking Time: 20 minutes

Ingredients:

- 16 cloves garlic, chopped
- 4 tablespoons fish sauce
- 2 tablespoons white sugar
- 4 tablespoons tapioca flour
- 4 tablespoons light soy sauce
- 1 teaspoon white pepper powder
- Vegetable oil, as required
- 2 pounds whole prawns, unpeeled, divided

Method:

1. Add garlic, fish sauce, sugar, tapioca flour, soy sauce, and pepper into a large bowl and stir.
2. Add prawns and coat them well in the mixture.

3. Place a heavy skillet over high heat. Add 2-3 tablespoons oil. Place prawns in a single layer in the skillet. Cook until the underside is brown and crisp. Flip and cook the other side .

4. Repeat the above step with the remaining prawns.

Peanut Chicken Satay with Peanut Dipping Sauce

Serves: 4

Nutritional values per serving:

Calories – 257, Fat – 12 g, Carbohydrate – 11 g, Protein – 28 g

Preparation Time: 15 minutes

Cooking Time: 2 hours 20 minutes (including refrigeration)

Ingredients:

<u>For chicken satay:</u>

- 2 shallots, minced
- ¼ cup canned light coconut milk
- ½ tablespoon raw honey
- 3 cloves garlic, finely chopped
- 1 tablespoon fresh lime juice
- A handful fresh cilantro, chopped
- 1/8 teaspoon turmeric powder
- ¼ teaspoon ground cumin
- 1 pound raw chicken breast, skinless, boneless, cut into 2 inch chunks
- 8 bamboo skewers, soaked in water for a couple of hours

<u>For peanut dipping sauce:</u>

- 1-2 tablespoons hot water
- 1 ½ tablespoons fresh lime juice
- 1 tablespoon low sodium soy sauce
- ¼ cup chunky peanut butter
- ½ tablespoon raw honey
- ¼ teaspoon chili sauce

Method:

1. To make chicken satay: Add shallots, coconut milk, honey, garlic, lime juice, cilantro, turmeric, and cumin into a blender and blend until smooth.

2. Pour into a large bowl. Add chicken and stir until well coated.

3. Refrigerate for 2 hours.

4. Meanwhile, make the peanut dipping sauce as follows: Add hot water, lime juice, soy sauce, peanut butter, honey, and chili sauce into a bowl and whisk until well combined.

5. Cover and set aside for a while for the flavors to set in.

6. Set a grill to preheat on high setting.

7. Insert the chicken on to skewers.

8. Grill until the chicken pieces are lightly charred on the outside and well-cooked inside. Turn the skewers every 2 minutes.

9. Serve chicken satay with peanut dipping sauce.

Vegetable Crisps with Peanut Dip

Serves: 8

Preparation Time: 10 minutes

Cooking Time: 40 minutes

Ingredients:

- 6 medium beetroots, scrubbed, thinly sliced
- 4 medium potatoes, scrubbed, thinly sliced
- 1 teaspoon sea salt flakes
- 4 tablespoons sunflower oil
- Peanut dipping sauce to serve – refer previous recipe

Method:

1. Place beetroots in one bowl and drizzle half the oil over it. Toss until well coated.

2. Place potatoes in another bowl and drizzle remaining oil over it. Toss until well coated.

3. Take 3-4 large nonstick baking sheets or line normal baking sheets with parchment paper.

4. Place the beets and potatoes on separate baking sheets in a single layer.

5. Sprinkle salt over the vegetables.

6. Bake in a preheated oven at 425°F until crisp. Flip sides every 10-15 minutes and rotate the baking sheets.

7. When done, cool completely on a wire rack.

8. Serve with peanut dipping sauce.

9. Leftover crisps can be stored in an airtight container.

Thai Fish Cakes with Lime and Honey Dipping Sauce

Serves: 4

Preparation Time: 15 minutes

Cooking Time: 40 minutes

Ingredients:

- 6 ounces floury potatoes, peeled, chopped into chunks
- 6 ounces haddock fillet
- 2 tablespoons lemon juice
- ½ thin lemongrass stalk, thinly sliced, lightly crushed
- 2 spring onions, thinly sliced
- A handful fresh cilantro, chopped
- 2 teaspoons Thai red curry paste
- 2 cloves garlic, chopped
- ½ teaspoon fresh ginger, finely choppe
- Juice of ½ limed
- 1 egg, lightly beaten
- 2 tablespoons plain flour
- 1.75 ounces fresh breadcrumbs
- 1 tablespoon extra-virgin olive oil
- Salt to taste

For lime and honey dipping sauce:

- ¼ cup lime juice
- ½ teaspoon fresh ginger, chopped
- ½ teaspoon Thai red curry paste or to taste
- 1 tablespoon honey
- 1 teaspoon soy sauce
- ½ fresh mild red chili, deseeded, thinly sliced

For salad:

- 1 small cucumber, chopped
- ½ bunch lettuce, finely shredded
- A handful fresh mint leaves, finely shredded

Method:

1. Add potatoes into a saucepan. Cover the potatoes with water. Place the saucepan over medium heat.
2. Cover with a lid and cook until soft. Drain and add into a bowl.
3. Mash with a potato masher.
4. Meanwhile, add fish into a shallow pan. Cover with cold water. Add 2 tablespoons lemon juice. Place the pan over medium heat.
5. When it begins to boil, lower heat and simmer for a minute. Turn off the heat and cool for 3-4 minutes. Drain off the lemon juice from the pan and discard

the skin and bones. Flake the fish with a fork and add into a bowl

6. Add potatoes, lemongrass, spring onions, cilantro, curry paste, garlic, ginger, and 2 tablespoons lime juice into the bowl of fish and mix well. Make 1-tablespoon portions of the mixture. Shape into cakes.

7. Place flour on a plate. Place bread crumbs on another plate.

8. First dredge the fishcakes in flour and next dip in the bowl of egg. Shake to drop off excess egg. Finally dredge in breadcrumbs and place on a tray.

9. Place the tray in the refrigerator for an hour.

10. Place a nonstick frying pan over medium heat. Add oil. Once the oil heats, place the fishcakes in pan and cook until the underside is golden brown. Flip and cook the other side until golden brown. Cook in batches if required.

11. Meanwhile, make dipping sauce as follows: Add lime juice, ginger, curry paste, honey, soy sauce, and red chili into a small saucepan.

12. Place the saucepan over medium heat. Let it heat for a minute. Turn off the heat. Stir and set aside for a while for the flavors to set in.

13. To make salad: Add cucumber, lettuce leaves and mint leaves into a small bowl and stir.

14. Place the fishcakes on a serving platter. Surround by salad. Serve with dipping sauce.

Chapter 3:

Rice and Noodles

Pad Thai (Noodles)

Serves: 6

Nutritional values per serving: 1-¼ cups

Calories – 360, Fats – 10 g, Carbohydrates – 54 g, Proteins – 15 g

Preparation Time: 15 minutes

Cooking Time: 20 minutes

Ingredients:

- 9 ounces wide dried rice noodles, cooked according to the instructions on the packet (also called Pad Thai noodles or straight cut)

- 3 tablespoons peanut oil or canola oil
- 5 cloves garlic, minced
- 3 large eggs, beaten
- 12 ounces small shrimp, peeled, deveined
- 6 cups mung bean sprouts
- ¾ cup scallion greens, sliced
- 3 tablespoons fish sauce
- 3 tablespoons brown sugar
- 6 tablespoons rice vinegar
- ¾ teaspoon red pepper flakes
- Lime wedges to serve (optional)
- 6 tablespoons peanuts, roasted (optional)

Method:

1. Cook the noodles following the directions on the package until al dente. Drain and set aside.
2. Place a wok over high heat. Add 1-½ tablespoons of oil. Once the oil heats, add garlic and sauté until golden brown in color.
3. Add eggs and scramble them. Cook for about 30 seconds.
4. Stir in the shrimp and remaining oil. Sauté until the shrimp turns pink.
5. Add noodles, mung bean sprouts, scallions greens, fish sauce, brown sugar, vinegar, and chili flakes. Stir well. Heat thoroughly.

6. Serve with rice, sliced cucumber, and cilantro vinaigrette.

7. Serve with roasted peanuts and lime wedges.

Vegetarian Pad Thai

Serves: 3

Nutritional values per serving:

Calories – 347, Fat – 9.6 g, Carbohydrate – 56.7 g, Protein – 10.9 g

Preparation Time: 10 minutes

Cooking Time: 20 minutes

Ingredients:

- ¼ pound wide rice stick noodles (banh pho)
- 1/3 cup chili sauce
- 1 tablespoon soy sauce
- 2 tablespoons packed brown sugar
- 1 tablespoon water
- ¾ teaspoon fresh ginger, peeled, grated
- ½ teaspoon Serrano chili, chopped
- 2 teaspoons vegetable oil
- 6 ounces extra firm tofu, cut into ½ inch cubes
- 1 small egg
- 1 large egg white
- 2 cloves garlic, minced
- 1 cup fresh bean sprouts
- ½ cup green onions, diagonally cut

- 4 tablespoons cilantro, chopped
- 2 tablespoons roasted peanuts, chopped
- 3 lime wedges

Method:

1. Cook the noodles following the directions on the package until al dente. Drain and set aside.

2. Add chili sauce, soy sauce, brown sugar, water, ginger, and chili into a bowl. Set aside.

3. Place a nonstick pan over medium heat. Add 1-teaspoon oil. Once the oil heats add tofu and cook until brown on all the sides. Remove tofu and place on a plate. Set aside.

4. Whisk together egg white and egg in a bowl.

5. Place the pan back over heat. Add 1-teaspoon oil. Once the oil heats, add garlic and sauté for a few seconds. Add beaten eggs and scramble them. Cook for 30 seconds.

6. Add chili sauce mixture and noodles. Sauté for 2 minutes.

7. Add tofu, bean sprouts, onions, cilantro and stir.

8. Heat thoroughly.

9. To serve: Serve noodles sprinkled with cilantro and peanuts along with lime wedges on the side.

Thai Curry and Pork Sesame Noodles

Serves: 6

Nutritional values per serving: 1-¾ cups

Calories – 407, Fat – 12 g, Carbohydrate – 57 g, Protein – 16 g

Preparation Time: 15 minutes

Cooking Time: 25 minutes

Ingredients:

- 12 ounces rice noodles
- 4-5 tablespoons toasted, dark sesame oil
- 1 ½ tablespoons garlic, minced
- 1 ½ teaspoons brown sugar
- 3 scallions, chopped
- 3 teaspoons fresh ginger, minced
- 3 tablespoons Thai curry paste
- 3 tablespoons low sodium soy sauce
- 12 ounces cooked pork tenderloin or boneless pork loin chop, cubed
- 1 ½ cups red cabbage, shredded
- 1 ½ cups green beans, chopped
- 1/3 cup fresh cilantro, chopped

Method:

1. Cook the noodles following the directions on the package until al dente. Drain and set aside.

2. Add sesame oil, garlic, brown sugar, scallions, and ginger into a saucepan.

3. Place the saucepan over medium heat. When the pan is heated, cook for 15 seconds. Turn off the heat.

4. Add curry paste and soy sauce and stir.

5. Add noodles, pork, cabbage, beans, and cilantro into a bowl. Add the heated mixture into it. Toss well.

6. Serve immediately.

7. The mixture can be made ahead of time and refrigerated until use.

Thai Noodles with Spicy Peanut Sauce

Serves: 4

Nutritional values per serving:

Calories – 318.4, Fat – 11.6 g, Carbohydrate – 46.1 g, Protein – 9.1 g

Preparation Time: 12 - 15 minutes

Cooking Time: 30 - 35 minutes

Ingredients:

For noodles:

- 6 ounces linguine
- 2 tablespoons sesame oil

For sauce:

- 1 cup frozen stir fry vegetables
- ¼ cup green onion, chopped
- ½ tablespoon fresh ginger, minced
- 1 ½ tablespoons garlic, minced
- 1 medium carrot, finely shredded
- 2 tablespoons creamy peanut butter
- 2 tablespoons honey
- 2 tablespoons soy sauce
- 1 ½ tablespoons rice vinegar

- 1 teaspoon chili garlic sauce or to taste

Method:

1. Cook the pasta following the instructions on the package until al dente. Drain and add it back into the pot.

2. Add 1-tablespoon sesame oil and toss well.

3. Place a heavy pot over medium high heat. Add 1-tablespoon oil. Once the oil heats, stir fry vegetables, green onion, ginger, garlic, and carrots and cook for 3-4 minutes.

4. Add peanut butter, honey, soy sauce, vinegar, and chili garlic sauce into a bowl and whisk until well combined.

5. Pour over the vegetables and stir-fry for a couple of minutes. Turn off the heat.

6. Add pasta and toss well.

7. Serve right away.

Stir-Fried Noodles with Chicken (Pad Thai Gai)

Serves: 4-6

Nutritional values per serving: 1 cup

Calories – 495, Fat – 17 g, Carbohydrate – 47 g, Protein – 44 g

Preparation Time: 12 - 15 minutes

Cooking Time: 35 - 40 minutes

Ingredients:

- 12 ounces Thai rice noodles
- 1 pound chicken breast or thigh, cut into bite size pieces
- 4 tablespoons vegetable oil
- 6 cloves garlic, minced
- ½ cup carrot, grated
- 2 eggs
- 4 cups fresh bean sprouts
- 2/3 cup peanuts or cashews, roughly chopped or crushed
- 1 cup fresh basil, chopped
- 4 green onions, thinly sliced

For stir fry sauce:

- 2/3 cup chicken stock
- 4 tablespoons fish sauce
- 6 teaspoon brown sugar
- 2 tablespoons soy sauce
- 4 tablespoons lime juice
- Chili flakes to taste

Method:

1. Cook the noodles following the directions on the package until al dente. Drain and set aside.
2. To make stir fry sauce, add chicken stock, fish sauce, brown sugar, soy sauce, lime juice and chili flakes into a bowl.
3. Place chicken in a bowl. Add about ¼ cup of the sauce mixture over it. Stir and set aside.
4. Place a wok or large nonstick pan over medium high heat. Add oil. Once the oil heats, add garlic and sauté until fragrant.
5. Add chicken and sauté for 2 –3 minutes. Add carrots and sauté for a couple of minutes. Add more of the sauce mixture if required.
6. Move the mixture in the wok to one side.
7. Crack the eggs in the center of the wok. Scramble the eggs quickly and mix with the carrot mixture until well coated with the eggs.

8. Add noodles and some more of the sauce. Toss well.

9. Add more sauce if required.

10. Stir in the bean sprouts and toss well. Cook for 2-3 minutes.

11. Sprinkle nuts, basil, and green onions on top.

12. Serve with lime wedges.

Pad See – Ew

Serves: 4

Nutritional values per serving: 15 ounces

Calories – 1557.4, Fat – 62.5 g, Carbohydrate – 186.8 g, Protein –57.4 g

Preparation Time: 12 - 15 minutes

Cooking Time: 30 minutes

Ingredients:

- 28 ounces dried rice noodles, soaked in water for 40 minutes
- ¾ cup cooking oil

- 12 cloves garlic, crushed
- 1 pound pork or chicken or beef, thinly sliced or 1 pound shrimp
- 6 cups Chinese broccoli or regular broccoli, chopped
- 8 eggs

For sauce:

- 6 tablespoons oyster sauce
- 4 tablespoons light soy sauce
- 2 teaspoons pepper powder
- 2 teaspoons sweet soy sauce
- 4 teaspoons sugar

Method:

1. Pour water (at room temperature) over the noodles to soak them. Let soak for 20-40 minutes or until soft.
2. Place a large wok over medium heat. Add ½ cup oil. Once the oil heats, add garlic and the meat you are using. Sauté for 2-3 minutes.
3. Drain and add noodles and sauté for 3-4 minutes.
4. Add broccoli and cook for a minute.
5. Mix together the sauce ingredients and add into the wok.
6. Move the meat and broccoli mixture to one side of the wok. Add remaining oil and egg and cook for a minute. Move the meat mixture back to the middle of the wok.

7. Mix egg with the meat mixture. Sauté for a minute.
8. Serve right away.

Vegetarian Rice Noodles with Basil

Serves: 2

Nutritional values per serving:

Calories – 384, Fat – 7 g, Carbohydrate – 70 g, Protein – 5 g

Preparation Time: 15 minutes

Cooking Time: 25 minutes

Ingredients:

- 6 ounces rice stick noodles
- 1 tablespoon peanut or vegetable oil
- ½ tablespoon garlic, minced
- ½ teaspoon minced hot chilies or crushed red pepper flakes to taste
- Salt to taste
- Freshly ground pepper to taste
- ½ teaspoon sugar
- 1 tablespoon nam pla (fish sauce) or to taste
- ½ tablespoon lime juice or to taste
- ¼ cup Thai basil, roughly chopped

Method:

1. Pour hot water over the noodles to soak them. Cover with a lid. Let isoak for 30 minutes or until soft.

2. Place a pot of water over medium heat. When it begins to boil, drain the water from the noodles and add into the pot. Drain after 30 seconds. Rinse and set aside.

3. Place a large wok over medium heat. Add ½ cup oil. Once the oil heats, add garlic and chilies and sauté for a few seconds until fragrant.

4. Increase the heat to high heat. Add noodles, salt, pepper and sugar and toss well.

5. Stir in nam pla and lime. Taste and add more seasonings if necessary.

6. Add basil and toss well.

7. Serve right away.

Thai-style Beef

Serves: 2

Nutritional values per serving:

Calories – 305, Fat – 12.5 g, Carbohydrate – 23.6 g, Protein – 23.2 g

Preparation Time: 15 - 20 minutes

Cooking Time: 35 minutes

Ingredients:

- 1 teaspoon Thai green curry paste
  1 ½ tablespoons soy sauce + extra to serve
- Juice of a lime
- ½ tablespoon toasted sesame oil
- 1 tablespoon fish sauce
- Lime wedges to serve
- 1 tablespoon vegetable oil
- 1 lean British rump steak, sliced
- 1 package (10.5 ounces) stir fry vegetables or freshly chopped mixed vegetables like carrots, spinach, baby corn, onions etc.
- 1 package (10.5 ounces) rice noodles, cooked in boiling water for 5 minutes
- A handful fresh cilantro or mint, chopped
- A handful cashew, toasted

Method:

1. Add curry paste, soy sauce, lime juice, sesame oil and fish sauce into a bowl. Stir and set aside.
2. Place a wok or pan over medium heat. Add vegetable oil. Once the oil heats add beef and cook for a couple of minutes.
3. Stir in the vegetables and cook for 2 minutes.

4. Stir in the noodles and the sauce mixture. Toss well. Heat thoroughly.

5. Sprinkle a little water if necessary. Turn off the heat.

6. Add cilantro.

7. Serve in bowls. Sprinkle cashew on top. Drizzle some soy sauce on top. Place lime wedges on top and serve.

Thai Shrimp Rice Noodle Salad

Serves: 6

Nutritional values per serving:

Calories – 335, Fat – 0.7 g, Carbohydrate – 61.7 g, Protein – 19.3 g

Preparation Time: 15 minutes

Cooking Time: 20 - 25 minutes

Ingredients:

- 12 ounces vermicelli rice noodles
- 1 ½ tablespoons canola oil
- 18 ounces raw shrimp, peeled, deveined
- Salt to taste
- Pepper to taste
- ¾ cup cucumber, thinly sliced
- 1/3 cup scallions, minced
- ¾ cup carrots, shredded
- ¾ cup red bell pepper, deseeded, thinly sliced
- 1/3 cup fresh cilantro, minced

For tamarind lime vinaigrette:

- 1/3 cup lime juice
- 3 tablespoons soy sauce

- 1 ½ tablespoons fish sauce
- 2 cloves garlic, grated
- 3 tablespoons tamarind paste
- 1 ½ tablespoons brown sugar
- 1 ½ tablespoons fresh ginger, minced
- 1 ½ teaspoons sambal oelek (optional)

Method:

1. Cook the noodles following the directions on the package until al dente. Drain and set aside.
2. Place a large skillet over medium- high heat. Add 1-½ tablespoons of oil and let it heat.
3. Season shrimp with salt and pepper and place the shrimp in a single layer. Cook for a couple of minutes. Flip and cook for 1-2 minutes or until done.
4. Turn off heat and transfer into a large bowl. Add noodles and toss well.
5. Meanwhile, make the vinaigrette as follows: Add all the ingredients into a bowl and whisk well. Cover and set aside for a while for the flavors to set in.
6. Add cucumber, scallion, carrot, and bell pepper into the bowl of noodles and toss well.
7. Pour dressing on top. Toss well. Taste and adjust the seasoning if necessary.
8. Serve.

Thai Glass Noodles

Serves: 4

Preparation Time: 15 minutes

Cooking Time: 25 - 30 minutes

Ingredients:

For the noodles:

- 2 chicken breasts or 1 ½ cups firm tofu for a vegetarian or vegan option, chopped into bite sized chunks
- 16 ounces bean thread noodles or thin rice noodles
- 4 tablespoons vegetable oil
- 6 cloves garlic, minced

- 2 shallots or ½ cup purple onion, minced
- 3 cups mushrooms, chopped
- 2 red bell peppers, diced
- ½ cup fresh cilantro, chopped

For stir fry sauce:

- 2/3 cup chicken stock or vegetable stock for vegetarian or vegan option
- 3 tablespoons fish sauce or soy sauce for the vegetarian or vegan option
- 2 tablespoons brown sugar
- 6 tablespoons soy sauce
- 2 tablespoons hoisin sauce
- Chili flakes to taste

Method:

1. To make stir fry sauce: Add all the ingredients of stir fry sauce into a bowl and mix well.

2. Put chicken or tofu into a bowl and pour ¼ cup of the stir-fry sauce over it.. Toss well. Cover and refrigerate until use.

3. Cook the noodles following the directions on the package until al dente. Drain and rinse with cold water. Pour 2 tablespoons oil over it. Toss well and set aside. Chop the noodles with scissors if you like shorter noodles.

4. Place a large skillet over medium- high heat. Add 2 tablespoons of oil and let it heat.

5. Add garlic and shallots and sauté for a minute. Add chicken or tofu and cook until done. If the chicken or tofu is getting stuck to the skillet, add a little more of the stir-fry sauce.

6. Stir in mushrooms and bell pepper and a little more of the sauce. Cook for a few minutes until tender.

7. Add noodles and most of the sauce and toss well.

8. Taste and add more of the sauce if necessary.

9. Sprinkle cilantro on top and serve.

Kao Pad
(Thai – Style Fried Rice)

Serves: 6

Nutritional values per serving:

Calories – 584.7, Fat – 16.9 g, Carbohydrate – 94.4 g, Protein – 12.4 g

Preparation Time: 15 - 20 minutes

Cooking Time: 25 - 35 minutes

Ingredients:

- 6 tablespoons vegetable oil
- 3 tablespoons garlic cloves, minced
- ¾ tablespoon fresh ginger, minced
- 5 cups mixed vegetables, chopped (use a mixture of any of the following: Carrots, green peas, bell pepper, bean sprouts blanched for a few seconds)
- 9 cups short grained rice, cooked
- 3 eggs, beaten
- 2 cups fresh tomatoes, chopped
- 3 tablespoons Thai chili sauce
- 3 teaspoons lime juice
- 3 tablespoons light soy sauce
- 3 scallions, diagonally cut

- Lime wedges for garnishing

Method:

1. Place a wok over high heat. Add oil. Once the oil heats, add garlic and ginger. Sauté until golden. Remove the ginger and garlic and keep aside. Let the oil remain in the wok.

2. Add vegetables to the wok. The hard ones like carrot first and the tender ones bean sprouts in the end. Stir-fry the vegetables. Remove the vegetables and keep aside.

3. In the same wok, add rice and stir-fry until nice and hot.

4. With your stirring spoon, make a well in the center of the rice.

5. Add the beaten eggs in the well. Cook a little, scramble the eggs, and cook until done. Mix the egg into the rice.

6. Add tomatoes and the golden garlic-ginger, which was kept aside.

7. Sauté for a while. Add all the vegetables, chili sauce, lime juice, and soy sauce. Mix well.

8. Garnish with scallions and lime wedges and serve.

Spicy Thai Rice

Serves: 6

Nutritional values per serving:

Calories – 128.3, Fat – 6.2 g, Carbohydrate – 16.4 g, Protein – 2.8 g

Preparation Time: 15 - 20 minutes

Cooking Time: 40 - 45 minutes

Ingredients:

- 1 ½ tablespoons sunflower oil or vegetable oil
- 2 medium onions, chopped
- Kosher salt to taste
- 3 cloves garlic, minced
- ½ - 1 teaspoon ground ginger
- 3 ¾ cups water
- 2 Thai dried chilies, chopped
- Freshly ground pepper to taste
- 1 ½ cups jasmine rice
- Juice of 1 ½ lemons
- 1/3 cup peanuts, toasted, chopped
- 6 basil leaves, cut into thin ribbons
- 1/3 cup fresh cilantro, chopped

Method:

1. Place a heavy bottomed pan (that has a tight fitting lid) over medium - high heat.

2. Add oil. Once the oil heats, add onions and salt and sauté until pink.

3. Add garlic and ginger and sauté for a few seconds until aromatic.

4. Add water, chili and salt and pepper and stir.

5. When it begins to boil, add rice.

6. When it boils again, reduce heat and cover with a lid. Simmer for about 20-25 minutes. Turn off the heat and let it sit for 10 minutes. Do not uncover while it is resting.

7. Add lemon juice and fluff with a fork.

8. Sprinkle peanuts, basil, and cilantro on top and serve.

Vegan Thai Pineapple Fried Rice

Serves: 6

Nutritional values per serving:

Calories – 458, Fat – 7 g, Carbohydrate – 84 g, Protein – 14 g

Preparation Time: 15 - 18 minutes

Cooking Time: 25 - 30 minutes

Ingredients:

For stir fry sauce:

- 6 tablespoons fresh lime juice

- 4 teaspoons Sriracha sauce or any other hot sauce
- 2 teaspoons Indian curry powder
- 8 tablespoons low sodium soy sauce
- 10 teaspoons coconut sugar
- 2 teaspoons Chinese five spice<u>or fried rice:</u>
- 2 tablespoons neutral oil
- 1 medium red onion, chopped
- 6 cloves garlic, minced
- 2 inches fresh ginger, peeled, minced
- 2 heads broccoli, cut into small florets, stem peeled, cubed
- 4 carrots, chopped, cut into bite size piece
- 1 small head purple cabbage, chopped
- 1 cup pineapple chunks
- 5 cups cooked rice, preferably starchy variety
- 2 green onions or scallions, chopped, to serves
- A handful peanuts or cashew, toasted, chopped, to serve

Method:

1. To make stir fry sauce: Add lime juice, hot sauce, curry powder, soy sauce, sugar and Chinese five spice into a bowl. Stir until the sugar is completely dissolved.

2. Place a wok over high heat. Add oil. Once the oil heats, add red onions and sauté until it is pink.

3. Add garlic and ginger. Sauté until fragrant.

4. Stir in the broccoli, carrot, and cabbage and sauté until the vegetables are crisp as well as tender.

5. Stir in the pineapple and rice.

6. Add stir-fry sauce and mix until well combined. Heat thoroughly. Stir occasionally.

7. Taste and adjust the hot sauce or soy sauce if necessary.

8. Sprinkle green onion and nuts on top and serve.

Kao Pan Krapao
(Thai Chicken Fried Rice with Basil)

Serves: 4

Nutritional values per serving:

Calories – 538.7, Fat – 17 g, Carbohydrate – 63.6 g, Protein – 30.5 g

Preparation Time: 15 minutes

Cooking Time: 20 - 25 minutes

Ingredients:

- 4 tablespoons vegetable oil
- 6 cloves garlic, minced
- 2 tablespoons fresh Thai red chili pepper, chopped
- 16 ounces chicken breasts, skinless, boneless, cut into bite size pieces
- 4 cups cooked rice, cold
- 2 tablespoons soy sauce
- 2 tablespoons fish sauce
- 2 tablespoons sugar
- 4 tablespoons shallots, chopped
- A handful fresh cilantro, chopped
- ¼ cup Thai basil or normal basil, chopped

Method:

1. Place a wok over high heat. Add oil. Once the oil heats, add garlic. Sauté until golden.

2. Stir in the chilies and chicken and cook until chicken is cooked through.

3. Stir in the rice, soy sauce, fish sauce, and sugar. Toss well.

4. Add shallots, cilantro, and basil and mix well. Cook for a minute and turn off the heat.

5. Serve with any of the extra sauce if desired.

Thai Yellow Fried Rice with Shrimp

Serves: 4-6

Preparation Time: 15 minutes

Cooking Time: 30 – 35 minutes

Ingredients:

- 6 tablespoons vegetable oil
- 6 cloves garlic, sliced
- 20-30 medium raw shrimp, peeled, deveined, thaw if frozen
- 4 tablespoons white wine or white cooking wine or sherry
- 4 eggs, beaten
- 8 cups cooked rice, cold, preferably a day old
- 2 cups frozen peas, thawed
- 6 spring onions, sliced
- 1 cup fresh cilantro, chopped

For stir fry sauce:

- 1 teaspoon shrimp paste
- 2 teaspoons sugar
- 1 teaspoon shrimp paste
- 2 teaspoons sugar
- ½ teaspoon ground white pepper

- 2-3 teaspoons chili sauce or to taste
- 3 tablespoons fish sauce
- 2 tablespoons soy sauce
- ½ - 1 teaspoon turmeric powder

Method:

1. To make stir fry sauce: Add all the ingredients of stir fry sauce into a bowl and mix well.
2. Place a wok over high heat. Add 4 tablespoons oil. Once the oil heats, add garlic and shrimp. Sauté until shrimp turns pink. This should take a couple of minutes.
3. Add a little wine if the shrimp are getting stuck.
4. Move the shrimp to one side of the wok.
5. Add remaining oil in the center of the wok. When the oil heats, add eggs and scramble it. Cook for a minute.
6. Add rice and peas and stir. Add sauce and mix until well combined and heated thoroughly.
7. Keep tossing while it is being thoroughly heated.
8. Taste and adjust the fish sauce if required.
9. Garnish with spring onions and cilantro and serve with Thai hot sauce if desired.

Chapter 4:

Thai Soups

Tom Yum Goong
(Thai Spicy Shrimp Soup)

The National Dish of Thailand

Serves: 2

Nutritional values per serving:

Calories –293.4, Fat – 9.9 g, Carbohydrate – 11.9 g, Protein – 39.8 g

Preparation Time: 15 minutes

Cooking Time: 15 - 20 minutes

Ingredients:

- ¾ pound medium shrimp, peel, deveined, retain the shells
- 2 stalks fresh lemongrass, chopped into 2 inch pieces
- ¼ cup fresh galangal or ginger, peeled, chopped
- 3 fresh kaffir lime leaves or zest of 3 lemons, grated
- ¼ cup canned straw mushroom, quartered
- ½ tablespoon fish sauce
- 1 tablespoon roasted red chili paste
- 1 Thai red chili
- ¼ cup green onion, chopped
- ¼ cup cilantro, chopped
- ½ tablespoon lime juice
- lime wedges
- 4 ¾ cups water
- 3 tablespoons roasted peanuts, chopped (unsalted)

Method:

1. Add 3 cups water into a soup pot Add the retained shrimp shells. Place the pot over low heat. Simmer for an hour.

2. Pour the broth through a wire mesh strainer placed over a bowl. Discard the shrimp shells.

3. Transfer the broth into a saucepan and place saucepan over medium heat. Add the remaining water.

4. When it begins to boil, add lemongrass, galangal, and kaffir leaves and simmer for 10 minutes. Strain.

5. Pour the strained broth back into the saucepan. Add mushrooms, fish sauce, chili paste, and chili. Add shrimp, green onions, and cilantro. Simmer for 3-4 minutes or until the shrimps are cooked. When cooked, remove the chili with a slotted spoon and discard it.

6. Add lime juice and stir.

7. Serve in soup bowls sprinkled with roasted peanuts and lime wedges.

Authentic Thai Coconut Soup

Serves: 4

Nutritional values per serving:

Calories – 314, Fat – 21.6 g, Carbohydrate – 17.2 g, Protein – 15.3 g

Preparation Time: 20 minutes

Cooking Time: 18 - 20 minutes

Ingredients:

- 1 can (14 ounces) coconut milk
- 1 cup water
- ½ inch piece galangal, thinly sliced
- 5 kaffir lime leaves, torn
- 2 stalks lemongrass, bruised, chopped
- ½ pound shiitake mushrooms, sliced
- ½ pound medium shrimp, peeled, deveined
- 1 ½ tablespoons fish sauce
- 2 tablespoons lime juice
- 2 tablespoons brown sugar

  ½ teaspoon curry powder
- 1 tablespoon green onion, thinly sliced
- ½ teaspoon dried red pepper flakes

Method:

1. Place a pot of water over medium heat. When it begins to boil, add shrimp and cook for a minute. Drain and place the shrimp aside.

2. Add coconut milk and water into a saucepan. Place the saucepan over medium heat.

3. When it begins to simmer, add galangal, lime leaves, and lemongrass. Let it cook for 5-6 minutes.

4. Pass the mixture through a wire mesh strainer placed over another saucepan. Discard the solids.

5. Place the saucepan over medium heat. Add mushrooms and simmer for 4-5 minutes.

6. Add shrimp, fish sauce, lime juice, brown sugar and curry powder and stir.

7. Heat thoroughly.

8. Serve soup in bowls. Sprinkle green onions and red pepper flakes.

Thai Chicken & Coconut Soup

Serves: 6

Nutritional values per serving:

Calories – 126, Fat – 3 g, Carbohydrate – 9 g, Protein – 15 g

Preparation Time: 15 minutes

Cooking Time: 25 - 30 minutes

Ingredients:

- 3 cans (14 ounces each) low sodium chicken broth
- 9-10 slices fresh ginger, unpeeled, crushed
- 3 whole cloves garlic, unpeeled, crushed
- 3 stalks fresh lemongrass, trimmed, cut into 2 inch pieces
- 3 fresh chili peppers like Serrano or jalapeno peppers, halved lengthwise, deseed if desired
- 12 ounces chicken breasts, skinless, boneless, trimmed
- ¾ cup light coconut milk
- 4 ½ tablespoons cornstarch
- 3-4 tablespoons lime juice
- 2-3 teaspoons fish sauce or low sodium soy sauce
  3 scallions, trimmed, sliced

- 1/3 cup fresh cilantro leaves, chopped
- 6 thin slices lime to garnish

Method:

1. Place a pan over medium heat. Add broth, ginger, garlic, lemongrass, and chilies into the pan.
2. When it begins to simmer, add chicken and cover with a lid.
3. Lower heat and cook until the chicken is done.
4. Remove chicken and place on your cutting board. When cool enough to handle, slice the chicken.
5. Meanwhile, raise the heat to medium heat and simmer the broth for 5 minutes.
6. Strain the broth through a wire mesh strainer and press the ginger, garlic, lemongrass, and chilies to remove maximum juices from them. Finally, discard the solids.
7. Add coconut milk and stir.
8. Add cornstarch, lime juice, and fish sauce into a bowl and whisk well.
9. Pour into the soup stirring constantly until it thickens.
10. Add the chicken back into the pan. Taste and adjust the lime juice or fish sauce.
11. Serve in soup bowls garnished with scallions, cilantro, and lime slices.

Gaeng Khae (Spicy Vegetable Soup)

Serves: 6

Nutritional values per serving: 1 cup

Calories – 126, Fat – 3 g, Carbohydrate – 17 g, Protein – 9 g

Preparation Time: 25 minutes

Cooking Time: 35 - 45 minutes

Ingredients:

For chili paste:

- 24 dried Japones chilies
- 12 cloves garlic peeled
- ¾ teaspoon salt
- ¾ cup shallots, minced
- 3 stalks lemongrass, minced
- 3 teaspoons red miso

For soup:

- 6 cups low sodium vegetable broth
- 3 tablespoons low sodium soy sauce
- ¾ cup turnip or fennel chopped into chunks
- 3 cups beet greens or turnip greens or kale
- ¾ cup mushrooms, sliced

- 1 ½ cups tofu, chopped into chunks
- 1 ½ cups arugula, chopped
- ¾ cup fresh mint leaves

  6 tablespoons parsley, coarsely chopped

Method:

1. To make chili paste: Place the chilies in a bowl. Pour boiling hot water over them. Let isoak for 30 minutes. Drain and finely chop the chilies.

2. Add garlic and salt into a mortar and pound with a pestle. Add one by one the rest of the chili paste ingredients, pounding after adding each ingredient. Finally pound the entire mixture into a thick paste.

3. To make soup: Pour broth into a saucepan. Place over high heat. Add soy sauce and chili paste and mix well. Add turnip, beet greens, and mushrooms.

4. When it begins to boil, lower heat to medium low and simmer for 5 minutes.

5. Add tofu and boil for a couple of minutes. Add arugula, mint, and parsley and simmer for a couple of minutes more.

6. Serve hot in soup bowls.

Khao Tom (Rice soup)

Serves: 6

Nutritional values per serving:

Calories – 153, Fat – 3 g, Carbohydrate – 21 g, Protein – 11 g

Preparation Time: 20 minutes

Cooking Time: 40 - 45 minutes

Ingredients:

- 4 cups chicken stock
- 2 cups water
- 1 ½ tablespoons fresh ginger, grated
- 2 shallots, minced
- 4 inch piece lemongrass or juice of a lemon
- 1 cup carrots, thinly sliced
- 1 cup pork or chicken or diced, cooked chicken
- 2 teaspoons fish sauce
- 2 cups cooked rice
- A handful fresh cilantro, chopped
- 2 green onions, sliced

Method:

1. Place a large pot over medium heat. Add stock and water.

2. When it begins to boil, lower heat. Add ginger, shallots, lemongrass, and carrots.

3. Simmer for 10 minutes. Add meat, fish sauce, and rice and simmer for 15-20 minutes.

4. Turn off the heat and discard the lemongrass piece.

5. Garnish with cilantro and green onions.

6. Serve in soup bowls.

Thai Rice Soup with Pork-Cilantro Meatballs

Serves: 3

Nutritional values per serving:

Calories – 406, Fat – 19 g, Carbohydrate – 35 g, Protein – 21 g

Preparation Time: 20 minutes

Cooking Time: 48 - 55 minutes

Ingredients:

For meatballs:

- 1 large cloves garlic, peeled
- ¼ teaspoons white peppercorns
- 1 tablespoon cilantro roots or stems, finely chopped
- ½ teaspoon soy sauce
- ½ pound ground pork
- ½ tablespoon oyster sauce

For soup:

- 3 cups light chicken stock
- ½ cup jasmine or long grain rice, rinsed
- 2 cups hot water

To finish:

- 3-4 eggs (optional)
- 1 inch pieces fresh ginger, peeled, cut into matchsticks
- A handful fresh cilantro leaves, packed
- Fish sauce or Sriracha sauce to drizzle

Method:

1. To make meat mixture: Add garlic, white pepper, and cilantro into a mortar and pound with a pestle until a coarse paste is formed.

2. Spoon the paste into a bowl. Add soy sauce, pork, and oyster sauce and stir. Cover and refrigerate for 1-8 hours.

3. To make soup: Add stock and rice into a pot. Place the pot over medium heat.

4. When it begins to boil, lower heat and simmer for 20-25 minutes. Stir occasionally.

5. Add 1cup hot water and stir. Simmer for 15-20 minutes.

6. Add 1 more cup of hot water and simmer until the rice is overcooked and is falling apart.Remove the meat mixture from the refrigerator and make small bite- size balls of the mixture and carefully lower the balls into the simmering soup.

7. Let it simmer until the meatballs have cooked through. It should take 2-3 minutes after all the meatballs have been added.

8. Serve a little soup in each of the soup bowls. Crack an egg into each bowl. Cover the eggs with more soup.

9. Garnish with ginger, cilantro, and fish sauce or sriracha sauce.

Hot-and-Sour Prawn Soup with Lemon Grass

Serves: 8

Nutritional values per serving:

Calories – 182, Fat – 2.3 g, Carbohydrate – 15.2 g, Protein – 27 g

Preparation Time: 18 minutes

Cooking Time: 25 - 30 minutes

Ingredients:

- 8 cups chicken stock
- 2 pounds tiger prawns, shelled, deveined but retain the shells and rinse them
- 6 stalks lemongrass
- 20 kaffir lime leaves, torn
- 2 cups straw mushrooms
- ½ cup lime juice
- A handful fresh cilantro, chopped
- 4 green onions, chopped
- 6 tablespoons fish sauce
- 2 green onions, chopped
- 8 red chili peppers, deseeded, chopped

Method:

1. Add chicken stock and prawn shells into a soup pot.
2. Slightly smash the lemongrass stalks and add into the pot. Add half the lime leaves.
3. When it begins to boil, lower heat and simmer. In a while, the lemongrass will change its color. Strain the stock through a wire mesh strainer and add it back into the pot. Discard the lemongrass, shells, and lime leaves.

4. Place the pot back over heat. When it begins to simmer, add prawns and mushrooms and cook until the prawns turn pink in color.

5. Add rest of the ingredients and let it simmer for a couple of minutes.

6. Taste and add more of the sauces if necessary.

7. Serve in soup bowls.

8. Sprinkle some more green onions if necessary.

Spicy Chicken Noodle Soup

Serves: 6

Nutritional values per serving:

Calories – 131, Fat – 3 g, Carbohydrate – 14.5 g, Protein – 7.9 g

Preparation Time: 20 minutes

Cooking Time: 12 - 15 minutes

Ingredients:

- 2 ½ cups chicken broth
- ½ cup water

- 2 green onions, chopped
- 2 large carrots, cut into 1 inch pieces
- 1 small onion, chopped
- 2 cloves garlic, chopped
- 2 large stalks celery, cut into 1 inch pieces
- ½ teaspoon pepper powder
- ¼ teaspoon salt or to taste
- ½ tablespoon curry powder
- 1 teaspoon poultry seasoning
- 1 teaspoon dried sage
- ½ teaspoon ground cayenne pepper
- ½ teaspoon pepper powder
- 1 teaspoon dried oregano
- ½ cup white wine
- 1 tablespoon vegetable oil
- 6 ounces dried rice noodles
- ½ fresh chili pepper, deseeded, chopped

Method:

1. Place a soup pot over medium heat. Add oil. Once the oil heats, add chicken and cook until brown.
2. Add rest of the ingredients except noodles and red pepper and stir.
3. When it begins to boil, lower heat to low heat. Cover with a lid. Simmer until chicken is tender.

4. Add red pepper and noodles. Cook until the noodles are al dente.

5. Serve in soup bowls.

Thai Pumpkin Soup

Serves: 8

Nutritional values per serving:

Calories – 305, Fat – 25 g, Carbohydrate – 20.9 g, Protein – 5.4 g

Preparation Time: 15 minutes

Cooking Time: 12 - 15 minutes

Ingredients:

- 2 tablespoons vegetable oil
- 2 tablespoons butter
- 2 cloves garlic, chopped
- 4 small fresh red chili peppers, chopped
- 8 shallots, chopped
- 2 tablespoons lemongrass, chopped
- 4 ¼ cups vegetable or chicken stock
- 8 cups pumpkin, peeled, diced
- 3 cups coconut milk
- 2 bunches fresh basil leaves, chopped

Method:

1. Place a soup pot over low heat. Add oil and butter. When butter melts, add garlic, chilies, shallots, and lemongrass and sauté until aromatic.

2. Add stock, pumpkin, and coconut milk and cook until tender.

3. Turn off the heat. Blend the soup either in a blender or with an immersion blender until the consistency you desire is achieved.

4. Add basil leaves and stir.

5. Serve hot in soup bowls.

Thai Tofu Soup

Serves: 8

Nutritional values per serving:

Calories – 385, Fat – 30 g, Carbohydrate – 21.4 g, Protein – 14h g

Preparation Time: 15 minutes

Cooking Time: 25 minutes

Ingredients:

- 2 tablespoons vegetable oil
- 2 packages (12 ounces each) extra firm tofu, chopped into small cubes
- 4 tablespoons Thai red curry paste
- 2 tablespoons garlic, grated
- 2 tablespoons ginger, grated
- 8 cups vegetable broth
- 2 tablespoons white sugar
- 8 ounces broccoli, chopped into bite size pieces
- 8 ounces mushrooms, chopped into bite size pieces
- 2 onions, chopped
- 8 ounces cauliflower, cut into bite size florets
- 2 cans (14 ounces each) coconut milk
- Salt to taste

- Pepper to taste

Method:

1. Place a large pot over medium heat. Add oil. Once the oil heats, add onions, ginger, garlic and sauté for a minute.
2. Add curry paste and cook until the onions are turning slightly soft.
3. Add coconut milk and vegetable broth.
4. When it begins to boil, add tofu and all the vegetables.
5. When it begins to boil, lower heat and simmer until the vegetables are cooked.
6. Add salt and pepper and stir.
7. Serve hot in soup bowls.

Chapter 5:

Thai Curries

Authentic Thai Red Curry with Chicken

Serves: 4

Nutritional values per serving:

Calories – 1099.6, Fat – 32.6 g, Carbohydrate – 179.4 g, Protein – 24.1 g

Preparation Time: 12 - 15 minutes

Cooking Time: 18 - 20 minutes

Ingredients:

- 1 ½ tablespoons oil
- 2 ½ tablespoons Thai red curry paste or more to taste
- ¾ cup chicken stock
- 1 ½ cans (14 ounces each) coconut milk
- ½ chicken bouillon cube
- ½ tablespoon lime or lemon juice
- ½ teaspoon dried basil, crushed
- 1 tablespoon sugar
- 4 sweet basil leaves
- 1 carrot, shredded
- 4-5 large cherry tomatoes, halved
- 2 green bell peppers, chopped into bite size pieces

- 1 small Japanese eggplant, cut into bite size pieces

  1 yellow onion, chopped into bite size pieces
- 2 chicken breasts, skinless, boneless, cut into bite size pieces
- 2 cups cooked Jasmine rice

  ½ teaspoon fish sauce (optional)

Method:

1. Place a Dutch oven or skillet over medium heat. Add oil. Once the oil heats, add curry paste and sauté for a couple of minutes.
2. Stir in the stock and coconut milk. Sprinkle chicken bouillon cube and mix well. Bring to a boil.
3. Add lemon juice, dried basil, sugar, sweet basil leaves, carrots, tomatoes, bell pepper, eggplant, and onion and stir.
4. When it begins to boil, lower heat and cook for 5 minutes. Stir in the chicken and cook until chicken is tender.
5. Divide the rice into 4 serving plates. Divide the curry and serve over the rice.

Spicy Thai Red Curry Beef

Serves: 8

Nutritional values per serving:

Calories – 334, Fat – 11.2 g, Carbohydrate – 36 g, Protein – 24 g

Preparation Time: 15 minutes

Cooking Time: 18 minutes

Ingredients:

- 2 cans (14 ounces each) light coconut milk, chilled
- 4 teaspoons dark brown sugar
- ½ teaspoon crushed red pepper
- 4 teaspoons fish sauce
- 3 cups red bell pepper, sliced
- 2 cups onions, thinly sliced

  1 ½ pounds beef tenderloin, thinly sliced
- 3 cloves garlic, minced
- 4 cups hot cooked rice to serve
- 3-4 tablespoons Thai red curry paste
- 2 cups fresh basil leaves
- Salt to taste
- 4 tablespoons lime juice
- Lime wedges to serve

Method:

1. Remove the thick coconut cream skim that is floating on the top of coconut milk and add the skim into a large skillet. Add curry paste and place the skillet over medium high heat.
2. When it begins to boil, add remaining coconut milk, sugar, red pepper, and fish sauce and stir.
3. When it begins to boil, let it simmer for 2 minutes. Stir constantly.

4. Lower heat to medium heat and add bell peppers and onions and cook for 4-5 minutes.

5. Stir in the beef and cook until tender. Stir a couple of times white it is cooking.

6. Turn off the heat. Add basil, salt and lime juice.

7. Divide the rice among individual serving plates. Spoon beef over it and serve with lime wedges.

Thai Pork Green Curry

Serves: 8

Nutritional values per serving:

Calories – 366.3, Fat – 17 g, Carbohydrate – 10 g, Protein – 33 g

Preparation Time: 20 minutes

Cooking Time: 25 minutes

Ingredients:

- 1 ½ pounds orange sweet potato, peeled, cut into 1.5 cm pieces
- 15.5 ounces canned coconut cream
- 1 cup boiling water
- 4 teaspoons olive oil
- 2.2 pounds pork fillet, cut into 1.5 cm pieces
- ½ cup green curry paste
- 7 ounces green beans, cut into 3 cm pieces
- 2 bunches broccolini, cut into 2 cm pieces
- 4 teaspoons brown sugar
- 2 tablespoons fresh lime juice
- 2 teaspoons fish sauce
- A handful fresh cilantro, chopped to garnish
- ½ cup cold water
- Steamed Jasmine rice, to serve

Method:

1. Take a microwave safe bowl and add sweet potatoes into it. Pour a little cold water over it.

2. Cover and microwave on high for 3-4 minutes or until it is nearly tender.

3. Drain the water and set aside.

4. Add coconut cream and boiling water into a bowl and stir.

5. Place a wok over high heat. Add oil. Once the oil heats, add pork and sauté until brown.

6. Stir in the curry paste and sauté for a minute until fragrant. Add coconut cream+ water mixture.

7. When it begins to simmer, add the vegetables and cook until the broccolini is tender as well as crisp.

8. Stir in the sugar, lime juice ,and fish sauce.

9. Spoon the pork curry equally into individual serving bowls. Garnish with cilantro and serve with rice.

Thai Yellow Chicken Curry

Serves: 4

Nutritional values per serving:

Calories – 543.1, Fat – 25.5 g, Carbohydrate – 69.4 g, Protein – 11.2 g

Preparation Time: 15 minutes

Cooking Time: 20 minutes

Ingredients:

- ¾ tablespoon canola oil
- 1 tablespoon yellow curry paste or to taste

- ½ pound chicken, skinless, boneless, washed, cut into bite size pieces
- 1 can (14 ounces) coconut milk
- ¼ teaspoon paprika
- 2 tablespoons fish sauce
- 1 tablespoon sugar or to taste
- Zest of 2 limes, grated, or 3 kaffir lime leaves, torn
- 1 medium potato, cubed
- 3 small carrots, chopped
- 1 small bell pepper of any color, cut into squares
- 1 small onion, chopped

Method:

1. Place a deep pan over medium heat. Add oil. Once the oil heats, add curry paste and sauté until aromatic.

2. Add chicken and mix well so the chicken is well coated. Cook for 2-3 minutes.

3. Stir in the coconut milk, paprika, fish sauce, sugar, and lime zest. When the mixture starts boiling, reduce the heat and simmer for 10 minutes.

4. Add potatoes and cook for 5 minutes. Add rest of the vegetables. Cook until the chicken and vegetables are tender.

5. Serve hot with steamed rice.

Massaman Beef Curry

Serves: 6

Nutritional values per serving:

Calories – 855.6, Fat – 48 g, Carbohydrate – 33 g, Protein – 73 g

Preparation Time: 15 minutes

Cooking Time: 45 minutes

Ingredients:

- pounds beef chuck steak, cubed
- 1 ½ teaspoons ground cinnamon
- 10 cardamom seeds, powdered
- 3 tablespoons sunflower oil
- 3 onions, chopped
- 3 cloves garlic, chopped
- 4-5 tablespoons Massaman curry paste or to taste
- 2 cups beef stock
- 2 cans (14 ounces each) coconut milk
- 1 ½ tablespoons palm sugar
- 3 tablespoons tamarind paste
- 4 teaspoons fish sauce
- 1.3 pounds potatoes, peeled, cut into 2 inch cubes

- 3 tablespoons peanuts, unsalted, roasted
- 5 tablespoons water
- 6 tablespoons lime juice
- 5-6 teaspoons garlic, crushed
- Salt to taste
- Thai basil, torn to garnish
- Cooked Thai jasmine rice to server

Method:

1. Sprinkle cinnamon and cardamom over the beef.

2. Place a large saucepan over medium high heat. Add half the oil. Once the oil heats add beef and cook until brown on all the sides. Remove beef with a slotted spoon and set aside in a bowl.

3. Place the saucepan back over heat. Add remaining oil. Once the oil heats, add onion and garlic and sauté until onions are translucent. Stir in Massaman paste. Sauté for a minute or so until it is aromatic.

4. Stir in the stock, coconut milk, sugar, tamarind, and fish sauce. Add beef and stir.

5. When it begins to boil, lower heat and cover partially with a lid. Simmer for about 40 minutes.

6. Stir in the potatoes and cook until done.

7. Uncover and let it simmer for 3-4 minutes.

8. Add peanuts and stir. Serve over rice with a salad made of cucumber, basil, chili and rice vinegar.

Thai Seafood Curry

Serves: 6

Nutritional values per serving:

Calories – 243.1, Fat – 11.5 g, Carbohydrate – 10.3 g, Protein – 25.5 g

Preparation Time: 15 minutes

Cooking Time: 25 - 30 minutes

Ingredients:

- 1 ½ pounds mixed seafood
- 1 ½ pounds shrimp, peeled, deveined
- 6 ounces Thai red curry paste
- ¾ teaspoon fresh ginger, minced
- 0.5 ounces thick coconut milk
  1
- 1 ½ teaspoons finely shredded lemongrass
- 6 red chilies, chopped
- 1 ½ teaspoons fresh garlic, minced
- ¾ teaspoon ground coriander
- ¾ teaspoon garlic powder
- ¾ teaspoon ground cumin

Method:

1. Place a skillet over medium heat. Add mixed seafood and sauté until it is nearly, but not fully cooked. Transfer into a bowl. Sprinkle salt over it.

2. Add shrimp into the same pan. Sauté until it is nearly, but not fully cooked. Transfer into the bowl of seafood.

3. Add curry paste and coconut milk into the same pan. Add seafood and shrimp and simmer for a few minutes.

4. Add rest of the ingredients and cook for a few minutes until the flavors are well blended.

Northern Thai Curry with Chicken and Peanuts

Serves: 8

Nutritional values per serving:

Calories – 364, Fat – 20.7 g, Carbohydrate – 23.2 g, Protein – 23.8 g

Preparation Time: 20 minutes

Cooking Time: 35 minutes

Ingredients:

- 6 large dried red chili peppers
- 1 teaspoon cumin seeds
- 1 teaspoon coriander seeds
- 1 teaspoon turmeric powder
- 1 teaspoon mace
- 1 teaspoon ground mace on list twice
- ¼ cup lemongrass, thinly sliced
- ¼ cup galangal, peeled, chopped
- Salt to taste
- 4 cloves garlic, chopped
- 4 teaspoons fermented shrimp paste
- 2 shallots, chopped

- 2 tablespoons fresh turmeric root, peeled, chopped
- 2 teaspoons fish sauce
- 6 tablespoons palm sugar
- 1 1/3 pounds chicken breast, skinless, boneless, cubed
- 4 cups water + extra to soak chilies
- 6 tablespoons lime juice
- 4 tablespoons vegetable oil

  1 cup peanuts, unsalted, roasted + 2 tablespoons extra to garnish

  4 tablespoons tamarind juice

Method:

1. Add chili peppers into a bowl. Pour enough water to cover the chilies. Let it soak for 10-15 minutes. Drain and chop the peppers.

2. Add cumin, coriander, turmeric and mace into a mortar and pound with a pestle until fine powder is formed.

3. Add lemongrass, galangal, salt, garlic, shrimp paste, shallot, and fresh turmeric into the mortar and pound along with the pounded spices into a paste.

4. Transfer into a large bowl. Add fish sauce and palm sugar and mix well.

5. Add chicken into the bowl and stir until the chicken is well coated. Refrigerate for 1-24 hours (as per your convenience).

6. Place a large skillet over medium heat. Add oil. Once the oil is heated add chicken and cook until it is not pink anymore.

7. Add water, ginger, peanuts, and tamarind juice and stir. Cook until the gravy is thick.

8. Sprinkle peanuts on top and serve.

Duck Legs in Green Curry

Serves: 8

Nutritional values per serving:

Calories – 1448, Fat – 108.1 g, Carbohydrate – 81.1 g, Protein – 49.2 g

Preparation Time: 15 minutes

Cooking Time: 30 minutes

Ingredients:

- 8 duck legs
- 2 small onions, minced
- 6 cloves garlic, minced
- 2 inch piece fresh ginger, minced
- 4 Serrano peppers, deseeded, minced
- 6 cans (10 ounces each) coconut milk
- 6 tablespoons Thai green curry paste
- 4 green onions, minced
- 4 kaffir lime leaves, torn
- tablespoons fish sauce
- 2 packages (12 ounces) thin rice noodles
- 2 tablespoons vegetable oil

- 1 bunch cilantro, chopped

Method:

1. Place a large skillet over medium high heat with oil. Sear the duck legs in batches by placing the duck legs with its fat side touching the bottom of the skillet.

2. Sear until golden brown. Flip sides and cook the other side until golden brown.

3. Remove duck legs with a slotted spoon and set aside in a bowl. Retain about 1/3 cup of the duck fat in the pan and discard the rest.

4. Add onions into the pan and sauté until pink.

5. Add garlic, ginger, and Serrano pepper and sauté for 3 minutes.

6. Remove coconut cream skim that is floating on the top from 2 cans and add into the pan. Also add curry paste and cook for a couple of minutes until aromatic.

7. Add remaining coconut milk in the cans, green onions, kaffir lime leaves and fish sauce and mix well.

8. Add the duck legs back into the pan.

9. Lower heat and simmer for 15-20 minutes.

10. Meanwhile, cook the noodles following the instructions on the package.

11. Add noodles into the pan and toss well.
12. Garnish with cilantro and serve right away.

Green Tofu Curry

Serves: 6

Nutritional values per serving:

Calories – 536, Fat – 37.9 g, Carbohydrate – 44.2 g, Protein – 23.2 g

Preparation Time: 15 minutes

Cooking Time: 35 minutes

Ingredients:

- 2 ¼ cups water
- 1 ½ cups raw basmati rice, rinsed, drained
- 4 ½ tablespoons sesame oil
- 1 ½ packages (14 ounces each) firm, water packed tofu, drained, cubed
- salt
- 1 ½ cans (10 ounces each) coconut milk
- 3 tablespoons green curry paste

Method:

1. Pour water into a saucepan. Place the saucepan over high heat.

2. When it begins to boil, lower heat and cover with a lid. Cook until all the water is absorbed.

3. Turn off the heat. Let it cool for a while. Fluff with a fork.

4. Place a large saucepan over medium heat. Add oil. Once the oil heats, add tofu and cook until light brown and crisp on all the sides. Sprinkle with salt. Remove from heat.

5. Place another saucepan over medium heat. Add coconut milk and bring to a boil.

6. Add curry paste and stir until well combined.

7. When it begins to bubble, lower heat and let it simmer for 5-6 minutes. Turn off the heat.

8. Divide rice into serving plates. Place tofu over the rice. Spoon the coconut milk mixture over it and serve right away.

Panang Vegetable Curry

Serves: 4

Nutritional values per serving:

Calories – 226.3, Fat – 10.2 g, Carbohydrate – 29.2 g, Protein – 8.4 g

Preparation Time: 15 minutes

Cooking Time: 45 minutes

Ingredients:

- 1 tablespoon vegetable oil
- 1 large shallot, sliced
- 1 tablespoon Panang curry paste
- 1 tablespoon ginger, peeled, chopped
- 1 1/3 cups canned coconut milk
- 1 cup vegetable stock
- 4 fresh or frozen kaffir lime leaves
- 1 dried red chilli de arbol
- 2 pounds kabocha squash, cut into wedges
- ½ pound carrots, chopped into ½ inch pieces diagonally
- 1 cup cauliflower florets
- 1 red bell pepper, chopped into ½ inch squares

- 2 tablespoons liquid tamarind concentrate or tamarind paste
- ¼ cup fresh basil, chopped
- 1 tablespoon soy sauce
- 6 ounces firm tofu, cut into 1 inch cubes
- ½ tablespoon fresh lime juice
- Kosher salt to taste
- ¼ cup roasted peanuts, chopped
- Steamed jasmine rice to serve

Method:

1. Place a heavy bottomed pan over medium heat. Add oil. Once the oil heats, add shallots and sauté until translucent. Add Panang curry paste and ginger and sauté for 2-3 minutes.

2. Add 3 tablespoons coconut milk and sauté until brown.

3. Stir in the remaining coconut milk, vegetable stock, kaffir lime leaves, and chili.

4. Add kabocha squash.

5. When it begins to boil, lower heat and cover with a lid. Cook until squash is nearly cooked. Remove squash with a slotted spoon and place in a bowl.

6. Add , carrots, cauliflower, and bell pepper into the pot. Place the squash on top of the vegetables and

cook until all the vegetables are tender. Do not stir while the vegetables are cooking. Remove squash and place on a plate.

7. Add tamarind liquid, half the basil, soy sauce, and tofu and lime juice into the pot. Cover and simmer for a few minutes. Add more stock if you like thinner gravy. Add salt to taste.

8. Serve hot in bowls. Serve with squash wedge, basil, and peanuts along with steamed Jasmine rice.

Chapter 6:

Thai Pork & Beef Recipes

Thai Pork Tenderloin

Serves: 4

Nutritional values per serving:

Calories – 622.2, Fat – 20.9 g, Carbohydrate – 12 g, Protein – 88.2 g

Preparation Time: 15 minutes

Cooking Time: 45 minutes

Ingredients:

- ½ cup soy sauce
- ½ cup white wine
- ½ teaspoon red pepper flakes
- 4 teaspoons fish sauce
- 2 teaspoons brown sugar
- 2 tablespoons fresh garlic, minced
- 2 tablespoons fresh ginger, minced
- ¼ cup fresh lime juice
- 3 ½ pounds pork tenderloin, halved lengthwise
- 4 teaspoons olive oil or peanut oil
- 1 tablespoon cornstarch mixed with 1 tablespoon water (optional)
- 4 green onions, thinly sliced, diagonally

- ¼ cup finely diced red pepper
- ½ cup fresh cilantro, chopped
- 2 tablespoons peanuts, roasted, chopped
- 4 lime wedges
- Steamed Jasmine rice to serve

Method:

1. Add soy sauce, wine, red pepper flakes, fish sauce, brown sugar, garlic, ginger and lime juice into large zip lock bag. Shake to combine.

2. Add the pork into the bag and seal the bag. Turn the bag to coat the mixture well onto the pork. Chill for 30-45 minutes. Turn the bag to coat a couple of times while it is chilling.

3. Remove the bag from the refrigerator and remove the pork from the bag. Set aside the marinade.

4. Place a large skillet over medium heat. Add oil. Once the oil heats add pork and cook until brown on all the sides.

5. Remove pork with a slotted spoon and place on a cutting board. When cool enough to handle, cut into 1 inch thick slices.

6. Meanwhile, add the retained marinade into the skillet and let it simmer for a few minutes.

7. Add the sliced pork and cook until the pork is cooked through. Add cornstarch mixture if using and stir constantly until thick.

8. Serve over steamed Jasmine rice, garnished with red pepper, cilantro, peanuts, and green onions. Serve with lime wedges.

Slow Cooker Thai Style Peanut Pork

Serves: 3

Nutritional values per serving:

Calories – 357, Fat – 20 g, Carbohydrate – 9 g, Protein – 35 g

Preparation Time: 15 minutes

Cooking Time: 6 hours 25 minutes

Ingredients:

- 1 pound pork loin chops, boneless
- ½ cup teriyaki sauce
- 1 tablespoon rice vinegar
- ¼ cup red pepper flakes
- ½ teaspoon garlic, minced
- ½ tablespoon cornstarch mixed with 1 tablespoon water
- 2 tablespoons creamy peanut butter
- 4 green onions, thinly sliced
- 2 tablespoons peanuts, roasted, chopped
- 2 teaspoons fresh lime juice
- Hot cooked rice to serve

Method:

1. Place pork chops into a slow cooker or a Dutch oven. Mix together in a bowl, teriyaki sauce, rice vinegar, red pepper flakes, and garlic. Pour over the pork.

2. Cover with a lid and place the pot over low heat. Cook until meat is tender. In a slow cooker, cook for 6-8 hours on Low option.

3. When done, remove the pork with a slotted spoon and place on your cutting board. When cool enough to handle, chop into bite size pieces.

4. Pour the liquid remaining in the pot into a small saucepan. Place the saucepan over medium heat.

5. When it begins to boil, add cornstarch mixture and stir constantly until thick.

6. Add peanut butter and stir constantly until well combined. Add pork and heat thoroughly.

7. Serve over rice, garnished with peanuts and green onions. Serve with lime juice sprinkled on top if using.

Lemongrass Pork & Spaghetti Squash Bowl with Peanut Sauce

Serves: 6

Nutritional values per serving: 3 ounces pork with ¾ cup squash, ¾ cup spinach & ¼ cup sauce

Calories – 440, Fat – 23 g, Carbohydrate – 25 g, Protein – 33 g

Preparation Time: 20 minutes

Cooking Time: 50 minutes

Ingredients:

- 3 tablespoons fresh ginger, minced
- 3 tablespoons light brown sugar
- 3 tablespoons fresh lemongrass, minced
- 3 tablespoons low sodium soy sauce
- 1 ½ tablespoons fish sauce
- 1 ½ pounds pork tenderloin, cut into ½ inch slices
- 1 spaghetti squash of about 3-4 ½ pounds, halved lengthwise, deseeded
- 1/3 cup water
- 4 ½ tablespoons peanut oil, divided
- 1 ½ pounds baby spinach

- ¾ cup light coconut milk

- 6 tablespoons smooth natural peanut butter

Method:

1. Add 1 ½ tablespoons ginger, brown sugar, lemongrass, soy sauce, and fish sauce into a large shallow bowl.

2. Add pork and stir to coat the mixture well onto the pork. Set aside for 20-30 minutes. Turn the pork slices a couple of times while it is marinating.

3. Take a large microwave safe dish and place the squash in it with the skin side facing up. Add 3-4 tablespoons water into the dish.

4. Microwave on high for 10 minutes or until tender. You can also bake in an oven at 400°F for about an hour or until tender.

5. Meanwhile, place a large skillet over medium high heat. Add 3 tablespoons oil and let it heat. Add 1 ½ tablespoons ginger and spinach and cook until spinach wilts.

6. Remove the spinach from the skillet and place in a bowl. Cover and set aside.

7. Wipe the skillet clean and place it back over medium high heat. Add remaining oil. Once the oil heats add pork along with the marinade and cook until brown on all the sides.

8. Remove pork with a slotted spoon and place over the spinach. Cover and set aside.

9. Add coconut milk, water and peanut butter into the skillet and stir well. Scrape the bottom of the skillet to remove any browned bits that may be stuck.

10. Heat for a minute.

11. Remove the spaghetti squash from the microwave and let it cool for a few minutes. Using a fork, scrape the flesh from the spaghetti.

12. Place ¾ cup squash in each bowl. Trickle 2 tablespoons sauce mixture over the squash.

13. Place 3 ounces pork and ¾ cup spinach in each bowl. Drizzle 2 tablespoons sauce in each bowl.

14. Serve.

Pad Krapow Moo (Thai Pork Stir-Fry with Green Beans, Red Pepper and Mint)

Serves: 4

Nutritional values per serving:

Calories – 582, Fat – 22 g, Carbohydrate – 63 g, Protein – 38 g

Preparation Time: 15 minutes

Cooking Time: 25 - 30 minutes

Ingredients:

- 2 cups of water
- 1 teaspoon salt

- 1 cup basmati rice
- 3 tablespoons olive oil
- 12 ounces green beans, trimmed, halved
- 4 scallions, chopped
- 2 red bell peppers, thinly sliced
- 4 inches ginger, peeled, minced
- 4 cloves garlic, sliced
- 20 ounces ground pork
- ¾ cup soy sauce
- 2 tablespoons honey
- Pepper to taste
- 1 ounce fresh mint leaves, chopped
- 4 cloves garlic, minced (on list twice)

Method:

1. Add 2 cups water into a pot. Add a teaspoon of salt. When the water begins to boil, add rice.

2. Lower heat and cover with a lid. Simmer until rice is cooked. Turn off the heat. Fluff rice with a fork.

3. Place a large saucepan over high heat. Add half the oil. Once the oil heats, add green beans, scallions, and bell pepper and sauté until it is light brown. Add salt and pepper and stir.

4. Remove with a slotted spoon and set aside in a bowl.

5. Lower heat to medium heat. Add remaining oil. Once the oil heats, add ginger and garlic and sauté for a minute until aromatic.

6. Raise the heat to medium high heat. Add pork. Cook until brown. Break it simultaneously as it cooks.

7. Add the cooked vegetables, soy sauce, and honey. Mix well. Add some more salt and pepper and stir.

8. Turn off the heat and add mint. Mix well.

9. Divide rice into serving plates. Spoon the stir-fry pork over it and serve.

Thai Roasted Pork Fillet

Serves: 6

Nutritional values per serving: Without stir fry vegetables

Calories – 150, Fat – 3.5 g, Carbohydrate – 1 g, Protein – 28 g

Preparation Time: 25 minutes

Cooking Time: 45 - 50 minutes

Ingredients:

- 3 tablespoons fresh cilantro, finely chopped
- 2 tablespoons light coconut milk
- 2 tablespoons red curry paste
- 3 teaspoons fresh lime juice
- 1.7 pounds lean pork fillets, trimmed of excess fat
- Olive oil cooking spray
- Steamed white long grain rice, to serve
- Lime wedges to serve

Method:

1. Add cilantro, coconut milk, curry paste, and lime juice into a glass bowl. Mix well.

2. Cover the bowl with cling wrap. Chill for 10-15 minutes.

3. Place a large skillet or pan over high heat. Spray with cooking spray.

4. When the pan heats, place pork on it and cook until brown on all the sides. Remove the pork and place on a roasting pan.

5. Roast in a preheated oven at 375°F for about 20 minutes or cooked through.

6. Remove the pork from the oven and cover loosely with foil. Let it sit for 5 minutes.

7. When cool enough to handle, cut the pork into slices across the grain.

8. Divide the rice into serving bowls. Place pork over the rice and spoon any of the cooked juices over it.

9. Serve with lime wedges. Serve with stir-fried vegetables.

Thai Beef

Serves: 3

Nutritional values per serving:

Calories – 183, Fat – 4.9 g, Carbohydrate – 20.4 g, Protein – 14.3 g

Preparation Time: 15 minutes

Cooking Time: 28 minutes

Ingredients:

- ¾ pound flank steak
- 1 tablespoon coriander seeds, coarsely crushed
- 2 tablespoons soy sauce
- 1 clove garlic, minced
- ¼ cup firmly packed dark brown sugar
- ½ tablespoon lime juice
- A pinch ground ginger

Method:

1. Freeze flank steak for 20 minutes. Slice the steak across the grain and place in a bowl.

2. Meanwhile, add coriander, soy sauce, garlic, brown sugar, lime juice, and ground ginger into a bowl and mix well.

3. Pour this mixture over the steak. Toss well so that the steak is well coated with the mixture.

4. Cover and set aside at room temperature for an hour.

5. Place the rack in the oven 6 inches away from the heat source.

6. Place the steak slices on the rack in a single layer. Broil in a preheated oven for 1-2 minutes if you like it cooked medium rare.

Spicy Beef and Pepper Stir Fry

Serves: 2

Nutritional values per serving:

Calories – 312, Fat – 16 g, Carbohydrate – 15 g, Protein – 26 g

Preparation Time: 15 minutes

Cooking Time: 20 minutes

Ingredients:

- ½ pound beef top sirloin steak, cut into thin strips
- ½ tablespoon fresh ginger, minced
- 2 cloves garlic, minced, divided
- ½ teaspoon salt, divided
- Pepper to taste
- ½ cup light coconut milk
- ½ tablespoon Sriracha sauce (Asian hot chili sauce)
- 1 tablespoon lime juice
- 1 tablespoon sugar
- ¼ teaspoon lime peel, grated
- 1 tablespoon canola oil, divided
- 1 small red onion, thinly sliced

- 1 medium sweet red pepper, cut into thin strips
- 1 small jalapeño pepper, deseeded, thinly sliced
- 2 cups fresh baby spinach
- 1 green onion, thinly sliced
- A handful fresh cilantro, chopped

Method:

1. Place beef in a bowl. Sprinkle ginger, 1 clove garlic, ¼ teaspoon salt and pepper over it. Toss well. Let it sit for 15 minutes.

2. Add coconut milk, chili sauce, lime juice, sugar, lime peel, and ¼ teaspoon salt into a bowl and whisk well.

3. Place a skillet over medium high heat. Add ½ tablespoon oil. Once the oil heats, add beef and sauté until it is not pink anymore. Remove beef with a slotted spoon and place in a bowl.

4. Add onion, red pepper, 1 clove garlic, and jalapeño. Sauté until the vegetables are crisp as well as tender.

5. Add coconut milk and stir. When coconut milk heats, add spinach and also the beef. Cook for a few minutes until the spinach wilts. Stir occasionally.

6. Garnish with green onions and cilantro and serve.

Thai Beef with Basil

Serves: 2

Nutritional values per serving:

Calories – 240, Fat – 12 g, Carbohydrate – 60 g, Protein – 25 g

Preparation Time: 15 minutes

Cooking Time: 30 minutes

Ingredients:

- 1 tablespoon vegetable oil, divided
- 3 cloves garlic, thinly sliced
- 1 red chili, thinly sliced, deseeded if desired
- Salt to taste
- Freshly ground pepper to taste
- ½ pound ground beef
- ¼ cup low sodium chicken broth
- 1 ½ cups fresh basil leaves, divided
- 1 medium carrot, cut into matchsticks
- 1 scallion, thinly sliced
- lime juice
- ½ tablespoon fish sauce like nam pla or nuoc nam
- 1 tablespoon low sodium soy sauce
- ½ teaspoon sugar
- Steamed rice to serve
- Lime wedges to serve

Method:

1. Place a skillet over high heat. Add ½ tablespoon oil. Once the oil heats, add garlic and ½ the chili and sauté until aromatic.

2. Sprinkle salt and pepper over the beef and place in the skillet. Cook until brown. Break it simultaneously as it cooks.

3. Stir in the broth and 1 cup basil. Mix until well combined. Cook for a couple of minutes until the basil wilts.

4. Add carrots, scallions, ½ tablespoon lime juice, and remaining basil, chili and oil into a bowl and toss well.

5. Add fish sauce, soy sauce, sugar and remaining lime juice into another bowl and stir until the sugar dissolves completely.

6. Serve rice over individual serving plates. Divide the beef over the rice. Divide the carrot mixture over the beef. Drizzle the sauce mixture over the carrots and serve with lime wedges right away.

Beef Satay

Serves: 3

Nutritional values per serving:

Calories – 638.1, Fat – 48.2 g, Carbohydrate – 13 g, Protein – 38.3 g

Preparation Time: 30 minutes

Cooking Time: 6 hours 30 minutes

Ingredients:

- 1 pounds rump steak, trimmed of fat

For marinade:

- 1 ½ tablespoons tomato paste
- 1 tablespoon tomato paste
- 2 teaspoons curry powder
- 1 teaspoon ground cumin
- ¼ teaspoon chili powder
- 1 small clove garlic, minced
- Salt to taste
- Pepper to taste
- ½ teaspoon soy sauce
- 2 ½ tablespoons oil
- 1 ½ tablespoons white vinegar
- ½ tablespoon water
- ½ teaspoon soy sauce

For satay sauce:

- 1 tablespoon butter
- 2 tablespoons peanut butter
- 3 tablespoons malt vinegar
- ½ teaspoon soy sauce
- Pepper to taste
- Salt to taste

- 1 ½ tablespoons oil
- 1 small onion, finely chopped
- ¼ teaspoon chili powder
- 1 ½ tablespoons sugar
- ½ cup water

Method:

1. Soak 3-4 bamboo skewers in water for 30 minutes just before grilling.
2. Slice the meat into strips of 2-½ inches thickness. Cut each of the strips into pieces of 5 mm.
3. Add all the ingredients of marinade except oil into a bowl and stir. Add meat strips into it and stir.
4. Let it marinate for 6-8 hours. Retain the marinade and insert the meat pieces on to bamboo skewers.
5. Grill on a preheated grill until it is cooked inside and golden brown outside. Baste the skewers with oil.
6. Serve with satay sauce.
7. To make satay sauce: Place a pan over medium heat. Add butter. When butter melts, add onion and sauté until golden brown. Add rest of the satay sauce ingredients and mix well.
8. Add the retained marinade and mix until well combined. Boil until the sauce mixture thickens.
9. The sauce can be served hot or at room temperature.

Weeping Tiger (Thai Marinated Beef)

Serves: 2

Nutritional values per serving:

Calories – 777.6, Fat – 51.8 g, Carbohydrate – 8.1 g, Protein – 66 g

Preparation Time: 20 minutes

Cooking Time: 45 minutes

Ingredients:

For weeping tiger:

- 2 cloves garlic, sliced
- 8 sprigs cilantro
- 2 teaspoons nam pla (Thai fish sauce)
- 3 teaspoons fresh green peppercorns, available at specialist stores
- 2 teaspoons sugar
- 2 teaspoons light soy sauce
- 1 pound sirloin steak

For chili sauce:

- 2 teaspoons Thai rice
- 6 teaspoons nam pla
- ½ teaspoon sweet chili paste

- 6 teaspoons lemon juice

Method:

1. To make weeping tiger: Add garlic and cilantro into a mortar and pound into a paste with a pestle.

2. Remove the paste from the mortar and add into a large bowl. Add fish sauce, peppercorns, sugar, and soy sauce and stir.

3. Add steak and mix until well coated. Rub the mixture into the steak. Cover and set aside to marinate for 20-30 minutes.

4. To make chili sauce: Place a small pan over low heat. Add rice and toast until golden brown. Turn off the heat. Transfer into a dry mortar and pound into a paste with a pestle.

5. Transfer into a bowl. Add fish sauce, chilies, lemon juice, and sugar and stir until the sugar dissolves completely. Set aside for a while.

6. Place on a preheated grill rack that is lightly greased and grill for 1-2 minutes per side or rare or for 3-4 minutes for fully cooked.

7. Place the steak on your cutting board. When cool enough to handle, cut into strips.

8. Serve steak slices on serving plates. Drizzle chili sauce over it and serve with rice.

Chapter 7:

Thai Chicken and Egg recipes

Thai Chicken

Serves: 8

Nutritional values per serving:

Calories – 466, Fat – 20.5 g, Carbohydrate – 16.8 g, Protein – 53.4 g

Preparation Time: 15 minutes

Cooking Time: 2 hours 45 minutes

Ingredients:

- 2 cups soy sauce
- 4 tablespoons hot pepper sauce
- 2 tablespoons fresh ginger, peeled, minced
- 16 cloves garlic, minced
- 4 pounds chicken thighs, skinless
- 2 tablespoons sesame oil
- 2 tablespoons brown sugar
- 1 cup water
- ¼ cup green onions, chopped
- 2 onions, sliced
- 8 tablespoons crunchy peanut butter
- Chopped chives to garnish

Method:

1. Add soy sauce, hot pepper sauce, ginger and garlic into a large bowl and stir until well combined.

2. Add chicken into the bowl and turn to coat in the mixture well. Cover the bowl with a lid and refrigerate for 1-2 hours.

3. Place a Dutch oven on medium heat and add oil. Once the oil heats, add brown sugar. Stir until it dissolves completely.

4. Stir in the onions and stir it for a few minutes until onions are translucent.

5. Add chicken (retain the marinade) and let it cook until it turns brown on all the sides.

6. Add marinade and water and stir.

7. When it begins to boil, lower heat and cook for 15-20 minutes.

8. Stir in the peanut butter and cook for another 10 minutes.

9. Serve chicken on individual serving plates. Spoon sauce over the chicken. Sprinkle chives on top and serve.

Gaeng Massaman Gai (Massaman Chicken)

Serves: 8

Nutritional values per serving: 18.4 ounces

Calories – 1250, Fat- 57.4 g, Carbohydrate – 160.2, Protein – 28.9 g

Preparation Time: 20 minutes

Cooking Time: 35 - 40 minutes

Ingredients:

- 6 cups coconut milk
- 2 pounds chicken breast
- 5-6 tablespoons Massaman curry paste
- 4 tablespoons peanuts, unsalted, roasted
- 6 medium Yukon gold potatoes, peeled, parboiled, cut into 2 inch cubes
- cardamom seeds
- 4 tablespoons palm sugar
- 5 tablespoons water
- 2 teaspoons fish sauce
- whole white pearl onions, peeled
- 6 bay leaves

- 2 inch cinnamon, roasted
- 2 tablespoons tamarind
- 6 tablespoons lime juice
- 5-6 teaspoons garlic, crushed
- Salt to taste
- Cooked Thai jasmine rice to serve

For Ajad:

- 8 tablespoons rice vinegar
- 1 cup cucumber, sliced
- 3-4 Thai red chili peppers, thinly sliced
- 2 teaspoons sugar
- 2 shallots, minced

Method:

1. To make Ajad condiment: Mix together rice vinegar, cucumber, chili pepper, sugar and shallots in a glass bowl. Cover and aside overnight for the flavors to set in.

2. Separate the coconut cream skim that is floating on the top of the cans as thick cream and the remaining is thin milk. You will get 4 cups of thick cream and 2 cups of thin coconut milk.

3. Place a saucepan over medium heat. Add the thin coconut milk and let it simmer. Add chicken. Simmer until the chicken is cooked.

155

4. Meanwhile, place a wok over medium heat. Add thick coconut cream. Just before it begins to boil, add Massaman paste and thin coconut milk. Sauté for a couple of minutes.

5. Add rest of the ingredients except rice.

6. Heat thoroughly.

7. Serve hot with jasmine rice and Ajad condiment on the side.

Authentic Thai Cashew Chicken

Serves: 8

Nutritional values per serving:

Calories – 369, Fat – 15.9 g, Carbohydrate – 25.8 g, Protein – 34.4 g

Preparation Time: 20 minutes

Cooking Time: 25 minutes

Ingredients:

- 2 tablespoons canola oil
- 2 large yellow onions, chopped
- 2 large yellow bell peppers, chopped

- 6 tablespoons ketchup
- 2 tablespoons soy sauce
- 2 teaspoons white sugar
- 4 tablespoons oyster sauce
- 2/3 cup chicken broth
- 2 teaspoons Thai garlic chili paste
- chicken breast halves, skinless, boneless, chopped into bite size chunks
- 12 ounces broccoli, chopped into florets
- 2 yellow squashes, chopped
- 2 zucchinis, chopped
- 12 ounces mushrooms, quartered
- 1 cup cashew nuts, unsalted

Method:

1. Place a skillet over medium heat. Add oil. Once the oil heats, add onions and bell peppers and sauté until onions are translucent.
2. Add ketchup, soy sauce, sugar, oyster sauce, broth, and chili paste and mix until well combined.
3. Add chicken, broccoli, squash, zucchini, and mushrooms and stir.

4. Lower heat and cover with a lid. Cook until chicken is cooked through and the vegetables are tender. Turn off the heat.

5. Add cashews and stir. Serve right away.

Thai Chicken Wrap with Spicy Peanut Sauce

Serves: 8

Preparation Time: 20 minutes

Cooking Time: 40 - 50 minutes

Ingredients:

- chicken breasts (6 ounces each)
- 2 tablespoons vegetable oil
- 2 tablespoons soy sauce
- 2 tablespoons grill seasoning

For salad:

- 1 cucumber, peeled, deseeded, halved lengthwise, thinly sliced crosswise at an angle
- 2 cups carrots, shredded
- ½ cup fresh basil leaves, torn
- scallions, sliced at an angle
- 1/3 cup fresh mint leaves, chopped
- 4 teaspoons sugar
- 4 tablespoons rice wine vinegar or white vinegar
- Salt to taste
- 2 tablespoons sesame seeds

For spicy peanut sauce:

- ½ cup chunky peanut butter, at room temperature
- 2 tablespoons rice wine vinegar or white vinegar
- 4 tablespoons soy sauce
- ½ teaspoon cayenne pepper
- 4 tablespoons vegetable oil
- flour tortillas (12 inches each)

Method:

1. Place a grill pan over high heat.
2. Add chicken, oil, and soy sauce into a bowl and toss well.
3. Place chicken on the grill pan and grill for 6 minutes. Flip sides and grill the other side for 6 minutes. Remove chicken from the pan and place on your cutting board. When cool enough to handle, slice the chicken at an angle.
4. Meanwhile make the salad as follows: Add cucumber, carrots, bean sprouts, herbs, sugar, vinegar, salt and sesame seeds into a bowl and toss well.
5. To make spicy peanut sauce: Add peanut butter, vinegar, soy sauce and cayenne pepper into a bowl and whisk until well combined. Add vegetable oil in a thin stream whisking simultaneously.

6. Warm the tortillas following the directions on the package. Divide the chicken and vegetables into 8 equal portions.

7. Place a wrap on a serving plate. Layer with one portion of vegetables and chicken. Spoon some spicy peanut sauce over it.

8. Wrap like a burrito.

9. Repeat the above 2 steps to make the remaining burritos.

Thai Egg and Shrimp Omelette

Serves: 2

Nutritional values per serving:

Calories – 421, Fat – 35 g, Carbohydrate – 4 g, Protein – 23 g

Preparation Time: 10 minutes

Cooking Time: 12 - 15 minutes

Ingredients:

- 4 eggs
- 2 green onions, finely chopped
- 2 shallots, chopped
- 4 tablespoons butter
- 4 tiger shrimp, minced
- 2 teaspoons lime juice
- 2 tablespoons soy sauce
- Salt to taste
- Pepper to taste
- 4 tablespoons butter

To serve:

- 1 tomato, cut into round slices
- 2 tablespoons fresh parsley, chopped

Method:

1. Whisk together eggs in a bowl. Add rest of the ingredients. Whisk well.

2. Place a frying pan over medium heat. Add 2 tablespoons of butter and let it melt.

3. Pour half the egg mixture on the pan. Flip sides when the underside is golden brown and cook the other side.

4. Carefully remove onto a plate. Top with tomato slices.

5. Sprinkle parsley and serve.

6. Repeat steps 2-5 to make the other omelet.

Pad Thai Egg Rolls

Serves: 5

Nutritional values per serving: 2 rolls

Calories – 170, Fat – 9.5 g, Carbohydrate – 15.1 g, Protein – 8.1 g

Preparation Time: 15 minutes

Cooking Time: 45 minutes

Ingredients:

- ounces extra firm tofu, cut into small cubes
- Cooking spray
- 2 cloves garlic, chopped
- 1 small onion, chopped
- ¼ cup green onions, chopped
- ¼ small head red cabbage, chopped
- 1 egg beaten
- 2 tablespoons peanut butter
- ½ tablespoon lime juice (optional)
- ½ teaspoon lime zest, grated (optional)
- ½ teaspoon soy sauce or to taste
- 1 tablespoon chili sesame oil or to taste

- ½ teaspoon tamarind paste or to taste
- 2 teaspoons chili garlic sauce
- 1 teaspoon peanut butter, divided, to seal
- eggroll wrappers

Method:

1. Place a few sheets of paper towels on a plate. Place the tofu over it. Place some more sheets of paper towels over the tofu. Let it sit for a while. Press lightly a couple of times for the moisture to drain.

2. Place a nonstick skillet over medium heat. Spray some cooking spray in the pan.

3. When the pan heats, add garlic and sauté for about a minute until it turns aromatic. Remove the garlic from the pan and place in a bowl.

4. Spray some more oil if required. Add onion and green onions into the same skillet. Cook for a few minutes soft. Transfer into the bowl of garlic.

5. Spray some more oil if required. Add red cabbage into the same skillet. Sauté for 3 minutes. Transfer into the bowl of onions.

6. Spray the pan with oil and crack the egg into it. Scramble the egg. Transfer into the bowl of onions and stir until well combined.

7. Add 2 tablespoons peanut butter, lime juice, lime zest, soy sauce, chili sesame oil and tamarind paste

into the bowl and mix until the vegetables are well coated with the sauce mixture.

8. Spread the eggroll wrappers on your countertop. Spread a little of the filling along the center. Fold the bottom and sides over the filling and roll the wraps.

9. Take a small bit of the peanut butter and place on the end part of the eggroll wrapper. Press the wrap to seal. (You are sealing with the bit of peanut butter).

10. Place the egg rolls on a baking sheet. Spray on top as well as sides of the egg rolls.

11. Bake in a preheated oven at 400°F for about 20 minutes or until the edges are light brown.

12. Serve hot.

Kai Jeow (Thai Style Fried Eggs)

Serves: 2

Preparation Time: 8 minutes

Cooking Time: 15 - 20 minutes

Ingredients:

- 4 tablespoons ground pork
- 2 teaspoons thin soy sauce
- 2 teaspoons ground white pepper
- 4 eggs
- 2 teaspoons fish sauce
- 4 tablespoons vegetable oil
- 2 tablespoons thinly sliced shallots
- 1 -2 red jalapeño pepper, thinly sliced
- 1-2 green jalapeño pepper, thinly sliced

Method:

1. Add ground pork, soy sauce, and white pepper into a bowl and mix well.
2. Add eggs and fish sauce into a bowl. Whisk until frothy.

3. Place a wok over medium high heat. Add half the oil. Once the oil heats, add shallots and peppers and sauté for 2-3 minutes.

4. Add pork mixture and sauté until cooked. Remove the pork from the wok and place in a bowl.

5. Place the work over high heat. Add remaining oil. When the oil is hot, add egg mixture.

6. Add the pork mixture back into the wok and mix until the eggs are well combined with the pork mixture.

7. Serve right away with hot Jasmine rice.

Thai Pork-Stuffed Omelette

Serves: 2

Preparation Time: 25 minutes

Cooking Time: 35 - 40 minutes

Ingredients:

<u>For pork:</u>

- 1 tablespoon peanut oil
- 1 small onion, finely chopped
- 2 cloves garlic, finely chopped
- 8.8 ounces minced pork
- 1 ½ tomatoes, chopped
- ½ tablespoon rice vinegar
- ½ tablespoon fish sauce
- ½ bird's eye chili, finely chopped
- 1.5 ounces baby peas
- 1 ounce water chestnuts, finely chopped
- 1 tablespoon tomato sauce
- 1 teaspoon sugar
- 1 teaspoon oyster sauce
- ¼ cup water
- 1 small spring onion, thinly sliced
- A handful fresh cilantro, chopped

- 1 tablespoon fried shallots, to serve

For salad:

- Zest of ½ lemon
- Juice of ½ lemon
- ½ tablespoon fish sauce
- ½ tablespoon sugar
- ½ bird's eye chili, thinly sliced
- 1 ½ Lebanese cucumbers, peeled, deseeded, cut into matchsticks

A handful cilantro leaves

- ½ long red chili, thinly sliced
- 1 small red onion, sliced

For omelet:

- 3 eggs
- ½ teaspoon fish sauce
- 1 small spring onion, thinly sliced
- ½ tablespoon peanut oil

Method:

1. To make salad: Add lime juice, lime zest, fish sauce, and sugar into a small bowl and stir until well combined.
2. Add rest of the ingredients of salad in a bowl. Pour fish sauce mixture over it and toss well. Cover the

bowl with cling wrap and set aside for a while for the flavors to set in.

3. Place a wok over medium high heat. Add oil. Once the oil heats add the onions and let them cook for about 2 – 3 minutes. Then add the garlic and cook for another 1 minute.

4. Add pork and sauté until it is nearly cooked. Add rest of the ingredients to pork and mix until well combined.

5. Cover the wok and cook for about 5 minutes. Turn off the heat.

6. To make omelet: Add eggs into a bowl and whisk well. Add fish sauce and spring onions and whisk well.

7. Place a medium pan over medium-high heat. Add half the oil. Once the oil heats, add half the egg mixture. Swirl the pan so that the egg spreads.

8. Cook until the underside is golden brown. Place half the pork mixture in the center of the omelet. Fold the sides over the mixture so that the pork is enclosed by the omelet.

9. Carefully remove the omelet and place on a plate with its seam side facing down.

10. Repeat steps 7-9 to make the other omelet.

11. Divide and serve salad on the side. Garnish with fried shallots on top and serve.

Chapter 8:

Thai Seafood Recipes

Grilled Shrimp with
Spicy Peanut-Lime Sauce

Serves: 4

Nutritional values per serving:

Calories – 535, Fat – 39.4 g, Carbohydrate – 14.9 g, Protein – 29.2 g

Preparation Time: 20 minutes

Cooking Time: 45 - 50 minutes

Ingredients:

For shrimp:

- 2 tablespoons lemongrass, minced, white part only
- 1 tablespoon garlic, minced
- 1 small Thai chili pepper or Serrano chili pepper, minced
- 2 tablespoons ginger, minced
- A handful fresh cilantro, chopped
- tablespoons peanut oil or canola oil
- 1 pound extra-large shrimp, peeled, deveined, with tail on

For spicy peanut lime sauce:

- tablespoons lime juice

- ¼ cup mirin (Japanese sweet wine)
- 1 tablespoon cold water
- 2 tablespoons rice vinegar
- 1 tablespoon dark soy sauce
- 1 ½ tablespoons lime zest, grated
- ½ tablespoon ginger, minced
- 1 fresh Thai chili pepper or Serrano chili pepper, deseeded
- 1 teaspoon fish sauce
- 4 tablespoons smooth unsalted peanut butter
- 1 teaspoon garlic, minced
- 1 tablespoon mint leaves, chopped
- 2 tablespoons peanut oil
- A handful fresh cilantro, chopped
- Salt to taste
- 2 tablespoons peanuts, roasted, chopped

Method:

1. Add all the ingredients of shrimp except shrimp into a bowl and mix well.
2. Add shrimp and mix until the shrimp are well coated with the mixture. Cover and set aside for 20-30 minutes.
3. Meanwhile, add lime juice, mirin, water, rice vinegar, soy sauce, lime zest, ginger, chili pepper, fish sauce,

peanut butter, and garlic into the food processor and pulse until smooth and well combined.

4. Transfer into a bowl. Add mint, cilantro, salt, and peanuts and mix well.

5. Drain the marinade. Shake the shrimp to drop off excess marinade and place shrimp on a preheated grill. Grill for about 2 minutes on each side.

6. Serve right away with spicy peanut sauce.

Barbecued Fish with Thai dressing and Coconut Rice

Serves: 2

Nutritional values per serving:

Calories – 485.4, Fat – 14.9 g, Carbohydrate – 50.6 g, Protein – 36.1 g

Preparation Time: 20 minutes

Cooking Time: 12 minutes

Ingredients:

- ½ cup Jasmine rice
- 4.5 ounces light coconut milk
- 2 firm fish fillets (5.3 ounces each)
- A few sprigs cilantro, to serve
- 1 teaspoon peanut oil
- pepper to taste

For Thai dressing:

- 1 tablespoon sweet chili sauce
- 1.5 cm piece ginger, peeled, finely grated
- 1 tablespoon lime juice
- ½ tablespoon soy sauce
- 1 small stick lemongrass, white part only, finely chopped

177

- 1 small clove garlic, crushed
- 1 teaspoon fish sauce
- ½ tablespoon peanut oil

Method:

1. To make Thai dressing: Add sweet chili sauce, ginger, lime juice, soy sauce, lemongrass, garlic, fish sauce, and oil into a small bowl. Whisk well.

2. To make fish and rice: Add rice, coconut milk and ¼ cup water into a saucepan. Place the saucepan over high heat and stir.

3. When it begins to boil, lower heat and cover with a lid. Simmer until rice is cooked. When done, fluff with a fork.

4. Brush oil over the fish. Sprinkle pepper.

5. Place on a charcoal grill or a barbecue grill over medium high heat. Cook for 3-4 minutes per side.

6. Serve fish with rice. Sprinkle cilantro on top and drizzle Thai dressing on top and serve.

Thai Shrimp Burgers

Serves: 8

Nutritional values per serving:

Calories – 479, Fat – 19.4 g, Carbohydrate – 33.1 g, Protein – 43 g

Preparation Time: 15 minutes

Cooking Time: 45 minutes

Ingredients:

- 3 pounds large shrimp, peeled
- ¼ cup ginger, minced
- 4 large cloves garlic, minced
- 2 jalapeño peppers, deseeded, minced
- ¾ cup cilantro, minced
- 1 cup Thai peanut sauce
- 1 teaspoon salt
- 1 cup dry breadcrumbs
- 4 tablespoons vegetable oil
- small (4 inches each) pita breads
- green onions, thinly sliced
- 4 tablespoons fresh lime juice
- 4 cups slaw mix

Method:

1. Add 1/3 of the shrimp into the food processor bowl and process until a paste is formed.

2. Add rest of the shrimp and pulse for a few seconds until the shrimp is finely chopped.

3. Place shrimp into a bowl. Add ginger, garlic, jalapeño, ½ cup cilantro, ½ cup peanut sauce, salt, and breadcrumbs and mix using a fork.

4. Divide the mixture into 8 equal portions and shape into patties of about 4 inches diameter.

5. Place on a plate and chill for 20-30 minutes.

6. Grill on a preheated grill until cooked through.

7. Remove the burgers and place on a plate. Place pita breads on the grill and grill for 1 minute on each side. Split each of the pita breads, crosswise.

8. Place burgers on half the pita halves. Place slaw on top of the burgers. Cover with the remaining pita bread halves.

Whole Fish Fried with Basil and Chilies

Serves: 8

Nutritional values per serving:

Calories – 338, Fat – 26.7 g, Carbohydrate – 9.2 g, Protein – 16.6 g

Preparation Time: 15 minutes

Cooking Time: 8 - 10 minutes

Ingredients:

- Oil, to deep fry

- 2 whole tilapias (10 ounces each)

For sauce:

- 2 tablespoons vegetable oil
- 2 yellow onions, chopped
- cloves garlic, peeled, chopped
- large red chili peppers, sliced
- 4 tablespoons fish sauce
- 4 tablespoons light soy sauce
- ½ cup Thai basil leaves or to taste
- ½ cup fresh cilantro, chopped

Method:

1. Make a few slits at an angle all over the fish. The slits should be up to the rib bones.
2. Make 2 lateral slits from head to tail on either side of the fins.
3. Pour enough oil into a large saucepan or deep fryer to deep fry the fish.
4. When the oil is well heated but not smoking, gently lower the fish into the oil. Fry until crisp on both the sides.
5. Remove fish with a slotted spoon and place on a plate that is lined with paper towels.
6. Repeat with the other fish.
7. Place a large wok or skillet over medium heat. Add 2 tablespoons oil. Once the oil heats, add onions,

garlic, and red chili pepper and sauté until light brown.

8. Stir in fish sauce and soy sauce and turn off the heat.

9. Add basil and cilantro and stir.

10. Pour sauce over the fish and serve.

Chili Crab

Serves: 8

Nutritional values per serving:

Calories – 226, Fat – 10.1 g, Carbohydrate – 21.1 g, Protein – 14.5 g

Preparation Time: 15 minutes

Cooking Time: 10 - 12 minutes

Ingredients:

- shallots, peeled
- red chili peppers
- whole crabs, cleaned, quartered
- 4 tablespoons vegetable oil
- cloves garlic, chopped
- 1 inch piece fresh ginger, chopped
- tablespoons ketchup
- 4 tablespoons white sugar
- 4 tablespoons vinegar
- Salt to taste
- Pepper to taste
- 4 eggs, beaten

- 2 tablespoons water or as required
- 1 large bunch fresh cilantro, chopped

Method:

1. Place shallots and red chili peppers into the food processor bowl and process until a smooth paste is formed.
2. Slightly break the claws and big legs of the crabs.
3. Place a large skillet over medium-high heat. Add oil. Once the oil heats add crabs and cook until it is cooked. The shells will change color.
4. Remove crabs with a slotted spoon and place on a plate.
5. Lower heat to medium low and add the shallot paste. Sauté for a couple of minutes until aromatic.
6. Add garlic and ginger and stir.
7. Add ketchup, sugar, and vinegar into a bowl and whisk well. Pour into the wok. Mix well.
8. Add the crab back into the wok and cook for 3-4 minutes.
9. Add salt and pepper to taste.
10. Add beaten eggs slowly, stirring constantly. If the sauce is very thick, add a little water.
11. Turn off the heat. Sprinkle cilantro on top and serve.

Coconut & Basil Steamed Mussels

Serves: 4

Nutritional values per serving:

Calories - 308, Fat – 15.1 g, Carbohydrate – 19.4 g, Protein – 25.5 g

Cooking Time: 25 minutes

Ingredients:

- 4 teaspoons canola oil
- ½ cup shallots, minced
- 4 teaspoons bottled garlic, minced
- 2 pounds mussels, scrubbed, de-bearded
- ½ cup fresh basil, torn
- 2 tablespoons fresh lime juice
- 2 teaspoons fish sauce
- 2 cups light coconut milk
- 1-2 teaspoons Sriracha sauce
- 2 teaspoons dark brown sugar
- 1 1/3 cups water
- 2/3 cup low sodium fat free chicken broth
- A handful basil, thinly sliced

For scallion rice:

- 1 cup Jasmine rice
- 2 cups water
- 2 teaspoons butter
- 2 green onions, thinly sliced
- ½ teaspoon kosher salt

Method:

1. Place a Dutch oven on medium heat. Add oil. Once the oil heats, add shallots and garlic and sauté until translucent. Add rest of the ingredients except sliced basil and scallion rice ingredients and stir

2. When it begins to boil, cover with a lid and cook for 4-5 minutes or until the mussels open up.

3. Remove the mussels with a slotted spoon and divide into 4 bowls. Cover and keep warm. Discard the unopened ones.

4. Let the mixture in the pot simmer for 4-5 minutes or until slightly thickened. Add 1 cup of sauce into each bowl.

5. Serve hot over scallion rice garnished with sliced basil.

6. To make scallion rice: Add all the ingredients of scallion rice into a saucepan. Place the saucepan over medium heat.

7. When it begins to boil, lower heat and cover with a lid. Cook until tender. When done, turn off the heat and let it sit for 5 minutes.

8. Fluff the rice with a fork.

Steamed Salmon Rolls with Spicy Seafood Dipping Sauce

Serves: 4

Preparation Time: 5 minutes

Cooking Time: 8 minutes

Ingredients:

- Chinese cabbage leaves
- 4 salmon fillets
- bird's eye chilies
- 2 tablespoons cilantro stems
- tablespoons lime juice
- cloves garlic
- tablespoons fish sauce
- 4 teaspoons sugar

Method:

1. Place a pot of water over medium heat. When it begins to boil, place the cabbage leaves in it for 30 seconds or until soft (the leaves should not break if rolled with a filling). Remove the cabbage leaves with tongs and set aside for cool for a few minutes.

2. Place 2 cabbage leaves next to each other, slightly overlapping each other. Place one fillet over it. Roll the cabbage leaves tightly enclosing the salmon. Place on a steamer basket.

3. Repeat the above step with the remaining cabbage leaves and salmon.

4. Steam the rolls in the steaming equipment you possess.

5. Cut into 1 inch slices and serve with a dip if desired.

Chapter 9:

Thai Vegetable, Tofu and Salad Recipes

Thai Basil Vegetables

Serves: 2

Nutritional values per serving:

Calories – 97.5, Fat – 5.5 g, Carbohydrate – 10.2 g, Protein – 4.1 g

Preparation Time: 20 minutes

Cooking Time: 8 minutes

Ingredients:

- 1 tablespoon fish sauce
- 1 teaspoon lime juice or to taste
- 1 teaspoon garlic, minced
- 1 teaspoon ginger, minced
- 1 tablespoon soy sauce
- 1 tablespoon sambal oelek chili paste or to taste
- 1 teaspoon sugar
- 1 medium zucchini, quartered, chopped
- 1 small carrot, slivered
- 1 cup mushrooms, sliced
- A handful fresh cilantro, chopped

193

- ¼ cup fresh basil, chopped
- ½ tablespoon corn-starch (optional)
- ¾ tablespoon vegetable oil

Method:

1. Add fish sauce, lime juice, garlic, ginger, soy sauce, sambal oelek, and sugar into a bowl and mix well. Add corn-starch if using and stir.
2. Place a wok over medium high heat. Add oil. Once the oil heats, add the vegetables and sauté for 3 minutes.
3. Pour in the sauce mixture and stir constantly until well combined. Cook until the vegetables are crisp as well as tender.
4. Add cilantro and basil and stir.

Thai Basil Tofu Stir Fry

Serves: 6

Nutritional values per serving:

Calories – 243, Fat – 13.6 g, Carbohydrate – 22 g, Protein – 13.6 g

Preparation Time: 15 minutes

Cooking Time: 10 minutes

Ingredients:

- 3 tablespoons brown sugar
- 3 tablespoons lime juice
- 1 teaspoon chili paste or to taste

- ½ tablespoon soy sauce
- 2 ½ teaspoons cornstarch (optional)
- 3 tablespoons vegetable oil
- 1 ½ teaspoons sesame oil
- 1 ½ pounds extra firm tofu, drained, pressed of excess moisture, cut into bite size pieces
- 1 ½ tablespoons ginger, grated
- cloves garlic, minced
- 3 red bell peppers, chopped
- 2 medium heads broccoli, cut into florets
- 3 cups fresh basil, sliced

Method:

1. Mix together in a bowl, brown sugar, lime juice, chili paste, soy sauce, and cornstarch.
2. Place a large skillet over medium heat. Add both the oils. Once the oil heats add tofu and cook until golden brown on all the sides. Transfer tofu on a plate.
3. Add ginger and garlic into the same pan and cook until fragrant.
4. Increase the heat to medium-high. Add vegetables and sauté until crisp as well as tender.

5. Stir in the lime juice mixture and mix well. Stir constantly until thick. Add tofu back into the pan. Add basil and stir. Heat thoroughly.

6. Serve over rice.

Thai Pork Salad

Serves: 3

Nutritional values per serving:

Calories – 218, Fat – 11.8 g, Carbohydrate – 9 g, Protein – 20 g

Preparation Time: 20 minutes

Cooking Time: 10 minutes

Ingredients:

- ½ pound lean pork chops, boneless
- Vegetable cooking spray
- ¼ cup fresh cilantro, chopped
- A handful fresh mint leaves, chopped
- 2 green onions, finely chopped
- ½ teaspoon fresh ginger, minced
- ¼ teaspoon ground red pepper
- ½ tablespoon fish sauce
- ¼ cup fresh lime juice
- ½ teaspoon sesame oil
- 2 tablespoons rice wine vinegar
- ½ tablespoon olive oil

- 1 tablespoon light soy sauce
- ounces broccoli slaw mix
- 1 medium cucumber, peeled, sliced
- Hot cooked basmati rice (optional)

Method:

1. Place pork in the food processor bowl and pulse until coarsely chopped.
2. Place a skillet over medium high heat. Spray with cooking spray. Add pork and cook until it is not pink anymore.
3. Turn off the heat. Drain the fat in the skillet. Add cilantro, mint, green onions, ginger, red pepper, fish sauce, lime juice and sesame oil and mix well.
4. Add vinegar, olive oil, and soy sauce into a bowl and mix well. Pour over the broccoli slaw and toss well.
5. Divide slaw among 3 serving plates. Divide and place pork over it. Divide the cucumber slices and serve.

Yam Nuea (Thai Beef Salad)

Serves: 4

Nutritional values per serving:

Calories – 658.5, Fat – 41.7 g, Carbohydrate – 23.1 g, Protein – 48.9 g

Preparation Time: 10 minutes

Cooking Time: 14 minutes

Ingredients:

- 2 pounds center cut beef tenderloin
- Freshly ground pepper to taste
- tablespoons freshly squeezed lime juice or to taste
- 1 teaspoons sugar or to taste
- tablespoons nam pla (fish sauce) or to taste
- 4 small Thai red chili peppers or 4 small Thai green chili, minced
- 1 cup shallots, thinly sliced
- 1 cup fresh cilantro leaves, chopped
- scallions, cut into ½ inch slices
- ¼ cup fresh mint leaves, finely chopped
- 2 cucumbers, cut into thin half moons

Method:

1. Cut the beef tenderloin into 2 halves horizontally to get 2 pieces of 1-inch thickness.

2. Sprinkle pepper on the pieces and rub it well into it.

3. Place on a preheated grill, on a greased rack for 5-8 minutes for medium rare.

4. Place beef on your cutting board. When cool enough to handle, slice the beef across the grain into very thin slices.

5. Meanwhile, add lime juice, sugar, fish sauce, and chilies into a large bowl. Stir until the sugar is completely dissolved.

6. Add the sliced beef, cilantro, scallions and mint into the bowl and toss well.

7. Place cucumber slices all around the edges of a serving platter.

8. Place beef on the center of the patter. Sprinkle cilantro on top.

9. Serve with rice on the side.

Thai Prawn Salad

Serves: 2

Nutritional values per serving:

Calories – 497, Fat – 18.7 g, Carbohydrate -59.4 g, Protein – 23.8 g

Preparation Time: 20 minutes

Cooking Time: 20 minutes

Ingredients:

- 1 avocado, peeled, pitted, sliced
- 1 small cucumber, cut into matchsticks
- 2 teaspoons fresh ginger, peeled, minced
- 12-15 green beans, trimmed, cooked
- 2 shallots, thinly sliced
- 2 cm piece lemongrass, finely chopped
- 2 red chilies, finely sliced
- 18-20 raw prawns, peeled
- tablespoons coconut cream
- Fish sauce to taste
- Juice of a lime
- Zest of a lime, grated

- Ready to eat rice noodles to serve

Method:

1. Place the avocado slices on a plate.
2. Add cucumber, ginger, beans, shallot, lemongrass, and chili into a bowl and toss until well combined.
3. Place the salad over the avocado slices.
4. Meanwhile, grill the prawns on a preheated grill and place over the salad.
5. To make dressing: Add coconut cream, fish sauce, lime juice and lime zest into a bowl and whisk well. Drizzle over the salad.
6. Serve with rice noodles on the side.

Conclusion

Thank you once again for purchasing the book.

Thai cuisine has gained fame across the world. From Africa to America, from Australia to Europe, there is no place on Earth where Thai cuisine is not known. This book contains delicious Thai recipes that are simple to prepare. The simplicity of the process does not change the taste of the dish. Any Thai dish, prepared at home or at a restaurant, tastes delicious. All you need to remember is to follow every step that has been written under each recipe word for word. This will ensure that your final dish tastes like a dish you may be served at a Thai restaurant.

Finally, if you enjoyed this book then I'd like to ask you for a favor. Will you be kind enough to leave a review for this book on Amazon? It would be greatly appreciated!

Click here to leave a review for this book on Amazon!

Thank you and good luck!

Bonus

As a way of saying thanks for your purchase, I'm offering a special gift that's exclusive to my readers.

Claim your bonus from the link below:

http://dingopublishing.com/heath-freebonus/

Another surprise! There are free sample chapters of our **favorite** book at the end (from page 209):

Anti-inflammatory Diet for Beginners
by Jonathan Smith

MORE BOOKS FROM US

If you want to find more books from us, visit our website at:

http://www.dingopublishing.com

Below is some of our favorite books:

INTERMITTENT FASTING

THE ULTIMATE GUIDE TO BURN FAT
AND BUILD LEAN BODY

JONATHAN SMITH

BURN FAT AND BUILD LEAN BODY FASTER WITH
HIGH INTENSITY INTERVAL TRAINING

JOSHUA KING

JAPANESE ETIQUETTE

The Essential Guide to Japanese
Traditions, Customs, and Etiquette

VINCENT MILLER

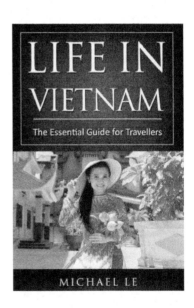

LIFE IN VIETNAM

The Essential Guide for Travellers

MICHAEL LE

Sample chapters:
'Anti-Inflammatory Diet For Beginner'
by Jonathan Smith.

Introduction

These days, everywhere you go and every website you visit, you are going to find discussions or adverts about this or that diet program. Diets that can help you lose weight, diets that can cure cancer, and even diets that promise to increase your bank account. Some of these diets work; others are a waste of your time, energy, and financial resources. The anti-inflammatory diet is nothing like these fad diets. This revolutionary diet draws upon a simple scientific and biographical logic guaranteed to work for you regardless of your circumstances.

The anti-inflammatory diet has many innate benefits including lowering your risk of heart diseases, protecting the bones, helping you maintain a healthy weight, and increasing your body's ability to absorb nutrients from the foods you eat and the drugs you take.

This book is a comprehensive guide that shall impart upon you everything you need to know about the anti-inflammatory diet. Let's begin.

Chapter 1:
Introduction to the Anti-Inflammatory Diet

To make this book easy to read and follow, we will start by understanding inflammation and the anti-inflammatory diet.

In its simplest terms, an anti-inflammatory diet simply refers to a collection of foods that have the ability to fight off chronic inflammation in your body.

So what exactly is chronic inflammation?

Well, before we discuss that, let's start by understanding what inflammation is first.

So what is inflammation?

Inflammation is simply a term used to refer to your body's response to infection, injuries, imbalance, or irritation with the response being swelling, soreness, heat, or loss of body function. It is the body's first line of defence against bacteria, viruses and various other ailments. The goal is to 'quarantine' the area and bring about healing/relief. This is the good inflammation, as it is helpful to your body. It is often referred to as acute inflammation. However, there are times when the inflammatory process might not work as expected resulting to a cascade of activities that could ultimately result to cell and tissue damage especially if it takes place over a prolonged period. This is what's referred to as chronic inflammation. This type of inflammation has nothing to do with injuries; it is not as a result of an injury or anything related to bacteria, virus or any other microbe. And unlike acute inflammation that comes with soreness, pain, heat and swelling, chronic inflammation comes with another set of symptoms some of which include diarrhoea, skin outbreaks, congestion, dry eyes, headaches, loss of joint function and many others. This inflammation is what you need to fight using an anti-inflammatory diet because if it is not addressed early, it might result to a number of various chronic health complications that we will discuss in a while.

So how exactly does this chronic inflammation develop that would actually require a diet to undo? Here is how:

It all starts in the gut. The gut essentially has a large semi-porous lining, which tends to fluctuate depending on various chemicals that it comes into contact with. For instance, if exposed to cortisol, a hormone that is high when you are stressed, the lining becomes more permeable. The lining also becomes a lot more permeable depending on the changing levels of thyroid hormones. This increased permeability increases the likelihood of viruses, bacteria, yeast, toxins and various digested foods passing through the intestines to get into the bloodstream, a phenomenon referred to as leaky gut syndrome (LGS). The thing is, if this (the intestinal lining becomes damaged repetitively), the microvilli in the gut start getting crippled such that they cannot do their job well i.e. processing and using nutrients with some enzymes that are effective for proper digestion. This essentially makes your digestive system weaker a phenomenon that results to poor absorption of nutrients. If foreign substances find their way into the bloodstream through the wrong channels, this results to an immune response that could result to inflammation and allergic reactions. This form of inflammation can bring about different harmful complications. What's worse is that as inflammation increases, the body keeps on producing more white blood cells to fight off the foreign bodies that have found their way into the bloodstream. This can go on for a long time resulting to malfunctioning of different organs, nerves, joints, muscles, and connective tissues.

Chronic inflammation is harmful to your body and your brain. Let me explain more of this:

Your body is responsible for supplying glucose to your brain so that your brain can perform optimally. When you eat too much inflammation-causing foods, your body slows down its process of transporting glucose to the brain since it concentrates on fighting off the inflammation. Your brain then keeps asking the body for glucose since it is not getting its fill. This effect causes you to crave sugary and pro-inflammatory foods. Inflammation can also result to abnormal levels of water retention along with other problems that contribute to stubborn weight gain. This just worsens the condition and causes your inflammation to worsen. Unfortunately, majorities of dieters focused on weight loss only focus on reducing calories and fatty foods but pay very little attention to how eating pro-inflammatory foods may be contributing to an inability to lose weight quickly.

If inflammation persists, it can bring about a wide array of health complications some of which include:

- Obesity and chronic weight gain

- Lupus

- Arthritis

- Cancer

- Diabetes

- Celiac disease

- Crohn's disease

- Heart disease

So how exactly does inflammation lead to disease? That's what we will discuss next.

How Inflammation Could Lead to Diseases

It is possible to have a disease-free body, but only if you can manage to keep your body balanced. Diseases develop only when something upsets the equilibrium (balance) of the body. An abnormal composition of blood and nymph is a typical example of such imbalance. These two are responsible for supplying the tissues with nutrients and carrying away eliminated toxins, metabolic by-products and wastes from the liver and kidneys. When you consume unhealthy meals, it may affect the balance of blood and nymph in the body and lead to inadequate supply of nutrients and thus, the body would be unable to give adequate support to kidney and liver function. The consequence of this is that it exposes the body to the risks of several diseases and inflammatory conditions, which I mentioned earlier.

Food Allergies, Food Intolerance, and the Anti-Inflammatory Diet

Food allergies happen when your immune system reacts to the proteins in certain foods. Your immune system releases histamines that may cause production of throat mucous, runny nose, watery eyes, and in severe cases, diarrhea, hives, and anaphylaxis.

Your immune system's reaction to food allergies is to trigger inflammatory responses because when a food causes allergic reaction, it stimulates the production of antibodies that bind to the foods and may cross-react with the normal tissues in your body.

One of the highpoints of the anti-inflammatory diet is that it calls for the elimination of foods that promote allergies and intolerance.

How the Anti-Inflammatory Diet Works

To cure and stop incessant inflammation, you must eliminate the irritation and infection, and correct hormonal imbalance by eating specific foods while avoiding others. This would help stop the destruction of cells and hyperactive response of your immune system. When on an anti-inflammatory diet, most of the foods you shall be eating have powerful antioxidants that can help prevent and eliminate symptoms of inflammation.

For instance, anti-inflammatory foods such as avocados contain Glutathione, a powerful antioxidant. Radishes contain Indol-3-Carbinol (13C), which increases the flow of blood to injured areas. Pomegranates have polyphenols that stop the enzyme reactions the body uses to trigger inflammation. Shiitake Mushrooms are high in polyphenols that protect the liver cells from damage. Ginger has hormones that help ease inflammation pain.

We will discuss more on the foods you should eat and those you should avoid later.

In the next chapter, we shall look at the basic rules of the anti-inflammatory diet as well as how to get the best out of the diet program.

Chapter 2:
Basic Rules of the Anti-Inflammatory Diet

As is the case with any diet, the anti-inflammatory diet has basic rules but as you are about to find out, these rules are very easy to follow and straightforward: no extreme rules that would leave you cravings-crazy and running back to a poor eating style after a few days.

When following this diet, there are about 11 rules you should follow:

1st: You Must Eat at Least 25 Grams of Fiber Daily

These should be whole grain fibrous foods such as oatmeal and barley, vegetables such as eggplant, onions, and okra, and fruits like blueberries and bananas. These fiber-rich foods have naturally occurring phytonutrients that help fight inflammation.

2nd: Eat at Least Nine Servings of Fruits and Vegetables Daily

A serving of fruit refers to half a cup of fruits while a serving of vegetable refers to a cup of leafy green vegetables. You could also add some herbs and spices such as ginger, cinnamon, and turmeric, foods that have strong anti-inflammatory and antioxidant properties.

3rd: Eat at Least Four Servings of Crucifers and Alliums Every Week

Crucifers refer to vegetables such as Brussels sprouts, Broccoli, mustard greens, Cabbage, and Cauliflower. Alliums refer to onions, garlic, scallions, and leek. These foods have strong anti-inflammatory properties and may even lower risks of cancer. You should eat at least four servings of these every day, and at least one clove of garlic daily.

4th: Consume Only 10% of Saturated Fat Daily

The average daily recommended calories for adults is about 2,000 calories every day. This means you have to limit your daily saturated fat caloric intake to no more than 200 calories. If you consume less than 2,000 calories daily, you have to reduce accordingly.

Saturated fats include foods like hydrogenated and partially hydrogenated oils, pork, desserts and baked goods, sausages, fried chicken and full fat diary. Saturated fats often contain toxic compounds that promote inflammation, which is why you need to eliminate these foods from your diet.

5th: Eat a Lot of Omega-3 Fatty Acid Rich Foods

Omega-3 fatty acids rich foods such as walnuts, kidney, navy and soybeans, flaxseed, sardines, salmon, herring, oysters, mackerel and anchovies are an essential part of this diet thanks to their strong anti-inflammatory properties.

6th: Eat Fish Thrice Weekly

It is important that you eat cold-water fish and low-fat fish at least three times a week because fishes are rich sources of healthy fats and can be great substitutes for saturated and unhealthy fats.

7th: Use Healthier Oils

The fact that you have to reduce your intake of some types of fat does not mean you should stop consuming all fats. You only need to reduce or even eliminate the consumption of unhealthy ones and limit your intake of healthy ones like expeller pressed canola, sunflower and safflower oil, and virgin olive oil. These oils have anti-oxidant properties that help detoxify the body.

8th: Eat Healthy Snacks at Least Twice Daily

Unlike in most diets, in this diet, you get to eat snacks as long as it is healthy. You can snack on healthy foods such Greek Yoghurt, almonds, celery sticks, pistachios, and carrots.

9th: Reduce Consumption of Processed Foods and Refined Sugars

Reducing your intake of artificial sweeteners and refined sugars can help alleviate insulin resistance and lower risks of blood pressure. It may also help reduce uric acid levels in your body. Having too much uric acid in your body may lead to gout, kidney stones, and even cancer. A high level of uric acid in the body is usually because of poor kidney function. Overloading your kidneys with pro-inflammatory foods may reduce kidney function and subsequently lead to excessive uric acid levels in the body.

Reducing your consumption of refined sugars and foods high in sodium can help reduce inflammation caused by excess uric acid within the body.

10th: Reduce Consumption of Trans Fat

Studies by the FDA reveal that foods high in trans-fat have higher levels of C-reactive protein, a biomarker for inflammation in the body. Foods like cookies and crackers, margarines, and any products with partially or fully hydrogenated oils are some of the foods with high trans-fat content.

11th: Use Fruits and Spices to Sweeten Your Meals

Instead of using sugar and harmful ingredients to sweeten your meals, use fruits that can act as natural sweeteners such as berries, apples, apricot, cinnamon, turmeric, ginger, sage, cloves, thyme, and rosemary.

Now that we have laid down the rules, the next thing we will do is to put what we've learnt into perspective i.e. what foods you should eat and what you should avoid. The next chapter has a comprehensive list of foods to consume and foods to avoid while on this diet. Consider printing out the chapter so you can use it as a reference each time you need to cook or make shopping decisions. If you do, it will not be long before you get used to the diet and can quickly decipher foods which foods you should and should not buy.

Anti-Inflammatory Diet For Beginner'

Find out more at:

http://dingopublishing.com/book/anti-inflammatory-diet-beginners/

Thanks again for purchasing this book.

We hope you enjoy it

Don't forget to claim your free bonus:

Visit this link below to claim your bonus now:

http://dingopublishing.com/heath-freebonus/

Printed in Great Britain
by Amazon

50039727R00129